P9-BAV-169

The Common Ground Dessert Cookbook

Recipes from the Common Ground Community Restaurant
Brattleboro, Vermont

Created, compiled and written by Katherine Kohrman
Graphics by Molly Forsythe and Meghan Merker
Hand lettering and cover by Meghan Merker
Additional writing by Kevin Connors

This cookbook is the product of the individuals who developed, tested
and compiled the recipes and created the artwork. It is also every bit
as much the product of the total Common Ground Collective, which
offers the supportive environment in which our many varied projects
can flourish.

Copyright © 1983 by the Common Ground Cooperative

25 Elliot Street · Brattleboro, Vermont · 05301

All rights reserved. No part of this book may be reproduced
in any form, except for brief reviews, without the written
permission of the publisher.

TEN SPEED PRESS

P.O. Box 7123 · Berkeley, California · 94707

Library of Congress Catalog Number : 83~40080

ISBN : 0~89815~113~9

Printed in the United States of America

10 9 8 7 6 5 4 3

The Common Ground Dessert Cookbook

Photo by John Willis

We dedicate this book to the original shareholders of the Common Ground, who had a vision of a community restaurant offer~ing wholesome food.

Over the years, through the tran~sition to a worker~owned cooperative, we hope we have remained true to that vision.

v

Thanks and Acknowledgements

We offer our loving thanks to friends and co~workers who have had a hand in creating these recipes : Bunny Al~corn, Virginia Bair, Karyn Brown, Kevin Connors, Sue Davidson, Bethleigh Flanagan, Helen Foreman, Molly For~sythe, Barbara Galson, Carol Graham, Fritz Hewitt, Claire LeMessurier, Bari Madwin, Meghan Merker, Larry Siegel, Charlotte Snyder, Robert Stack, Stanley Tayler, Kathleen Vetter, Jean Wagner.

For help in testing and perfecting these recipes : Karyn Brown, Carol Graham, Claire LeMessurier, Larry Siegel.

For co~ writing the Introduction, About the Common Ground, About the Cook~book, Glossary of Ingredients, Sweet~eners, Baking Hints and Converting Recipes sections : Kevin Connors.

For writing the Preface : Mollie Katzen.

For constructive criticism and proof~reading : Karyn Brown, Mollie Kat~zen, Bari Madwin.

vi

For typing the rough draft, JoAnn Golden; for indexing, Frances Bowles.

For encouragement and support: The Brattleboro Food Co-op, Stephen Green, Rachael Merker, Small Meadows Farm.

The artists would like to acknowledge those whose training and work have inspired ours : Scot Borofsky, Lisa Chang, Tim Cowles, Gerald Gedekes, Carol Graham, Hiro Kawasaki, Con Merker, K.K. Merker, Eleanor Simmons, Keith and Bernie Wallaur.

For her immeasurable help in editing and for passing on her knowledge and love of cooking, Margery Kohrman.

And finally, a special thank-you to the Common Ground Collective, for inspiring, encouraging and supporting individual initiative and for living with a crowded kitchen and with piles of artwork and recipes around the restaurant. Out of that seeming confusion has emerged this book.

~ The Cookbook Committee : Kevin, Molly, Katherine, Claire and Meghan

Preface

This is a wonderful, large selection of dessert recipes developed with great love and enthusiasm by a group of gifted, experienced bakers in Brattleboro, Vermont ~ the heart and soul of Maple Country. Whereas most collections of naturally ~ sweetened whole ~ grain recipes emphasize what one Should or Should Not eat in order to be a healthier, purer person, the approach here is joyful, light ~ hearted and sensual. "Natural" desserts have gained a sort of stodgy reputation among connoisseurs, probably because it is really difficult to work with these heavier ingredients and come up with an ethereal result. (And don't most of us want ethereal results?) At best, most people have turned to such concoctions out of feelings of duty and remorse, but for the real fun we tend to return to the trusty old white sugar ~ white flour routines. This book offers a departure from the cumbersome results of humdrum whole wheat dessert recipes. With much experimentation, the Common Ground bakers have discovered a broad range of textures, weights (ethereal included) and subtleties of flavor ~ all without compromising their commitment to pure ingredients. And they generously share their fine results in a most inviting and appealing presentation.

~ Mollie Katzen

Introduction

Desserts are fun, both to make and to serve. They make people happy. The enthusiasm shown and the praise so often expressed for sumptuous finales will do wonders for any cook's spirits. And don't forget to treat yourself to a beautiful dessert as well, when you need a little extravagance in your life.

As a restaurant we are proud of our desserts and we are excited to share them with you. The recipes in this collection are not merely organic versions of overly sweet desserts; nor are they the stereotype of heavy, bland "health food" desserts. We like granola as much as anyone (in fact, we offer our own granola recipes). But we have also discovered how to turn whole-some ingredients into light and elegant indulgences like our tortes and Bavarian creams.

We have replaced the overpowering sugar taste of many traditional desserts with a sweetness we find fuller and more flavorful. But taste buds dulled by white sugar and overprocessed foods may take a while to re-awaken to these subtleties. At the Common Ground and in these recipes we celebrate the various flavors and textures of whole grains and natural sweeteners.

About the Common Ground

The Common Ground, established in 1971, is the oldest natural foods res~taurant in New England. We are a collectively owned and run workers' cooperative. Our fifteen members share the responsibilities, frustra~tions, joys and profits of working to~gether and running a business.

We serve only whole, unrefined, un~adultered, unprocessed food. We pre~pare our food from scratch, using lo~cal products whenever possible. We use no white flour or white sugar; these refined ingredients rob dishes, especially desserts, of much of their flavor. Whole grains add a nut~like quality and a subtle sweetness which complements the delicate taste of nat~ural sweeteners. Whole foods offer virtually limitless flavor and texture variations as well as added nutritional value. Up to 80% of the nutrients pre~sent in wheat are lost in the milling, processing and bleaching of white flour and only four of the dozens of minerals and vitamins removed are returned to "enriched" white flour.

Our choice to serve whole foods goes further. As individuals, and as a restaurant, we can no longer ignore the hunger of the world. Globally, more than enough food is produced to provide an adequate diet for everyone. The problem lies in the unequal distribution of food wealth and food resources, and in the waste inherent in overprocessing.

Each one of us eating rationally will not end world hunger. But hopefully it will help us see our own part in the global food chain and will be a step in our own empowerment to take the larger steps necessary to create a more just world. As a restaurant we take the opportunity to address these issues concretely by attempting to offer, through positive example, a rational way of feeding ourselves.

It is a challenge for a large group to run a business collectively: to decide together what kinds of foods to serve, to set goals and to see them through. Creating a cohesive food philosophy which we present to the public through what we serve is an ever~evolving process. Over the years we have seen ourselves grow and change both individually and as a collective, and have developed a deep love for one another and for our work.

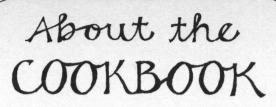

About the COOKBOOK

The recipes in this book range from very simple and quick to fairly com~ plex and time~consuming. They are di~ vided into eleven sections. There are desserts that will add splendor to any dinner party, as well as brownies, puddings, cookies and tea cakes for a light snack. There are candies and other goodies perfect for a children's party. We also offer recipes for wholesome muffins and other break~ fast sweets to start the day. In ad~ dition, frostings, fillings, toppings and crusts are included to use with these or any other recipes.

We have grouped most of the desserts that do not contain dairy products in their own section for the convenience of those who, out of choice or necessity, limit their intake of dairy foods. For a complete list of non~dairy recipes, check the index. Also see the index for desserts to fit other special dietary needs, such as wheat~free or salt~free.

Preparation times are noted at the top of each recipe for added conven~

ience. These are meant as guidelines only. Each individual cook knows his or her own work speed. For extra clarity these preparation times are broken down into their component parts: prep., baking, chilling, cooling, freezing and rising. "Prep" indicates all actual work time, including preparing other recipes such as crusts, fillings and frostings which complete a dessert. The other times are listed to indicate how far in advance preparations should begin.

Preheating instructions, pan size and pan preparation information are also given at the top of each recipe. Any time that a reference is made to another recipe, the page number is given for easy referral. We have standardized our use of common abbreviations:
T. = tablespoon ; t. = teaspoon ;
c. = cup ; 1b. or 1bs. = pound (s);
oz. = ounce(s) ; doz. = dozen ;
min. = minutes ; hr. = hour(s);
prep. = preparation ;
opt. = optional.

Included in the beginning of this book is a glossary of ingredients, which explains the few less common ingredients used in these recipes. It also provides useful information about familiar ingredients that will help make creative efforts more successful. There are also sections dealing with sweeteners, baking hints, and the art of converting white sugar ~ white flour recipes to recipes using whole foods.

   The graphics on these pages were designed to complement the recipes and to inspire you to uncover your own creative talents. With these recipes and simple hints you can serve desserts that are elegant, as well as healthful and delicious.

Table of Contents

* designates recipes which are found in the Non~Dairy Section.

1

2

Non~Dairy Sweets

Muffins

Breakfast Sweets

Glossary of Ingredients

Success with these desserts depends on the use of fresh, wholesome ingredients, and on understanding their characteristics. Some of the ingredients we specify may be unfamiliar to those unaccustomed to cooking with natural foods. All are available in natural food stores and many are now found in supermarkets as well.

Agar-agar ~ a vegetable gelatin made from seaweed. It produces a lighter gel than gelatin and can replace it in any recipe. It is available in many forms; we recommend buying flakes if possible. Bars and strands can also be grated into flakes in a blender or food processor. In powdered form agar-agar is much more concentrated and cannot be substituted equally in these recipes. Dissolve agar-agar flakes in water, fruit juice or other liquid by simmering it on moderate heat for 5~10 minutes, whisking occasionally until smooth.

Apples ~ There are many varieties of apples. For desserts, choose a good baking apple such as Cortland, Northern Spy or Jonathan.

Arrowroot ~ The most delicately-flavored thickening agent with the most nutritional value. Always dissolve in a cold liquid before using. Cornstarch can be substituted.

Barley Malt Syrup ~ See Sweeteners, page 13.

Bran ~ The outer layer of any grain; it is removed in processed flours. Bran is an important source of fiber.

Butter ~ These recipes call for lightly~salted butter unless otherwise noted. A natural additive-free margarine may be substituted.

Buckwheat Flour ~ A flavorful flour, heavier than whole wheat flour and low in gluten.

Cardamon ~ A delightful Indian spice. For the freshest flavor and aroma buy the pods whole and grind them as needed. (See page 17.)

Carob ~ Often described as a chocolate substitute, carob has its own distinctive flavor. It is naturally sweet and needs little added sweetener. Carob is available as chips and as a powder. Sift the powder before using it.

Chocolate ~ Use unsweetened baking chocolate in these recipes.

Cocoa ~ Use unsweetened cocoa.

Coconut ~ Read the label carefully on packaged coconut. Use unsweetened coconut with no preservatives, when available.

Cornmeal ~ Use unrefined yellow cornmeal. It is much more flavorful and nutritious than refined cornmeal, and the bran in it adds a slightly crunchy texture.

Dried Fruit ~ Use unsulphured, unsweetened dried fruit when available.

Extracts ~ Use pure almond, lemon, mint, orange and vanilla extracts with no additives. Available at most large supermarkets and health food stores.

Flour ~ See Baking Hints, pages 15~17, and About the Common Ground, page x.

Ginger Root ~ A versatile root. Fresh or powdered, it adds a delightful zing to many des~

serts. Keep fresh ginger root refrigerated.

Graham Crackers ~ Use 100% whole wheat, honey~sweetened crackers when available. The flavor is quite different from that of refined graham crackers.

Granola ~ A whole grain breakfast cereal and snack food. Shop around for a good crunchy variety, or make your own.

Honey ~ See Sweeteners, pages 11~13.

Jams, Jellies and Preserves ~ If available, use honey~sweetened jams, jellies and preserves, or try cider jelly, a Vermont product containing only apple cider.

Maple Syrup ~ See Sweeteners, pages 11~13 and Mail Order Maple Syrup, page 14.

Molasses ~ See Sweeteners, pages 11~13.

Oil ~ For desserts use a very light~flavored oil. This is important for oiling pans as well.

Peanut Butter ~ Natural peanut butter contains ground roasted peanuts and nothing else.

Rolled Oats ~ The whole grain of oat, flattened by rollers. Do not substitute instant oats.

Rice ~ Use brown rice.

Salt ~ Most table salt now contains chemicals and sugar. Read labels carefully when shopping.

Tahini ~ A rich sesame seed paste.

Tofu ~ A soybean cheese also known as bean curd. Tofu is high in protein, and when used as an egg substitute it makes light, nutritious non~dairy desserts. Tofu comes in blocks that are either soft or firm. Our recipes call for firm tofu. Soft tofu can be substituted by increasing the amount of tofu by 1~2 oz. and decreasing the liquid by the same amount.

Wheat Germ ~ The germ extracted from wheat, high in B vitamins and other nutrients. Use raw wheat germ if available, as it tends to be fresher. Always keep wheat germ refrigerated.

Whole Wheat Flour ~ See Baking Hints, pages 15~17, and About the Common Ground, page X.

For more details, see Additional Glossary and Baking Hints, pages 15~22.

sweeteners

The bags of white sugar on supermarket shelves are labelled "Pure Cane Sugar" ~ but white sugar is pure in a chemical sense only. It is processed and refined until it is 99.9% sucrose, leaving no trace minerals, no vitamins, no variety, no flavor; nothing but sweetness and empty calories. The same is essentially true of brown sugar and so-called "raw" sugar. Some of the nutrients removed in processing are necessary for proper metabolism. Thus the body must deplete its own stores to aid digestion.

White sugar is fairly inexpensive, in part because half of the sugar consumed in the U.S. is produced in the Third World by workers who often are not paid a living wage. At the Common Ground, we have chosen to make our desserts with natural sweeteners because, although they are more expensive, they are politically and nutritionally more palatable, and more flavorful as well. We use no refined sugar ~ white, brown, "raw" or powdered. The local availability and the delicate flavor of

maple syrup make it our choice sweetener. In our recipes, we use Fancy Grade light amber maple syrup, but a darker, less expensive grade of syrup can be used in most cases with equal success.

Vermont winters are often hard, but they help to create those special few weeks in March known as "sugaring season". There may still be three feet of snow on the ground, but the combination of warmer days and cold nights starts the sap running in sugar maple trees. Steam and wood smoke rise from the sugar houses as sap is boiled down to make that choicest of all syrups ~ pure maple syrup.

It takes 40 gallons of sap to make a single gallon of syrup, so maple syrup can be fairly expensive. If it is too expensive, or is not available, honey may be substituted in equal quantities. Honey flavors vary greatly; for baking, choose a light~flavored variety. Many recipes combine maple syrup and honey, producing desserts that are neither overly expensive nor dominated by the honey flavor.

Some of our recipes call for natural sweeteners other than maple syrup or honey. The unsulphured blackstrap molasses we use has a stronger flavor and is higher in iron and other nutrients than the light or dark molasses found in most supermarkets. Blackstrap molasses and honey both contain chromium, a vital nutrient missing in the typical American diet. Because of its strong flavor, use blackstrap molasses sparingly, combined with other sweeteners.

Barley malt syrup, available in most natural food and health food stores, has a light caramel flavor. It is less expensive, thicker, and a touch less sweet than maple syrup or honey, and can be substituted for them in many recipes. Barley malt syrup produces a caramel~like texture when boiled, and makes wonderful candies.

We also use fresh and dried fruits and fruit juices to sweeten desserts. Some~ times they serve as the only sweetening and other times are used in combina~ tion with other sweeteners. The fruity flavor enhances the sweetness in the finished product. For a more concentrated sweetener we use undiluted, un~ sweetened frozen orange juice concentrate or boiled~down fruit juices.

Mail Order Maple Syrup

Here is a list of several Vermont farms that will ship maple syrup anywhere in the United States. Prices vary with the season; write or call for details.

Goodell Farm ~ Quality maple syrup since 1840; all sizes.
RFD 3 · Box 170 · Putney, Vermont 05346
802·387·5345

Sidelands Sugarbush ~ Quality maple products, wholesale or retail.
RFD 3· Box 267· Putney, Vermont 05346
802· 387· 6611

Vermountain Farm ~ Quality maple syrup, maple sugar and maple cream.
P.O. Box 422 · Saxton's River, Vermont 05154
802· 869· 2671

Walker Farm ~ Pure maple syrup with that old~fashioned flavor.
RFD 2· Box 109· Putney, Vermont 05346
802· 254· 2476

Collin's Tree Farm
RFD 3· Putney, Vermont 05346
802· 387· 5757

Whole Wheat Flour ~

100% whole wheat flour is now readily available, even in supermarkets. The wonderful flavor and nutritional value of fresh-ground flour is lost, however, when it sits on a shelf for months.

When possible, buy it fresh from a local co-op or natural food store. Buy small amounts and store it in the refrigerator.

Whole wheat pastry flour differs from whole wheat bread flour, and understanding the difference can help in choosing the right flour. Bread flour is made from a "hard" wheat which has a high gluten content ~ ideal for yeasted breads. Pastry flour is made from a softer wheat with a much lower gluten content ~ ideal for

Additional Glossary and Baking Hints

pastries and other desserts, especially when ground finely. Most recipes in this book call for pastry flour. Substituting bread flour will produce a heavier, breadier result.

Handle pastry dough and batters as lightly as possible. Kneading, beating and stirring cause the gluten molecules in flour to join together, giving elasticity to a dough. Yeasted bread recipes rely on this elasticity to trap gas produced by the yeast, thus making the dough rise. Avoid developing this elasticity and subsequent toughness in desserts by mixing quickly but gently with as few strokes as possible.

Sifting flour separates and surrounds each particle with air, making it lighter. This is especially helpful with whole wheat flour, which is heavier than white flour. Always measure flour after sifting, and avoid packing it back down into the measuring cup. For the lightest cakes and tortes, and when using flour as a thickening agent in a sauce or custard, sift out and discard the coarsest flakes of bran.

Chilling Dough ~

Because of the use of liquid natural sweeteners, whole food pastry and cookie doughs often require extra chilling to facilitate handling. Chill dough thoroughly and work it quickly. If possible, roll dough out on a moveable surface which can be placed in the refrigerator if the dough becomes unmanageably soft. Chill unbaked pastry again before brushing with an egg wash so that the brush doesn't tear or disturb the shape of the pastry.

Pastry Crusts ~

Handling and temperature are both important in making a flaky pastry crust, especially with whole wheat flour. Overhandling will cause the gluten to develop, creating a tough crust. Chill all ingredients and the mixing bowl before starting. On a warm day, consider freezing the butter first.

Refrigerate dough for at least half an hour before rolling. Dough can be made up one or two days in advance. Roll out the dough lightly and with as few strokes as possible; do not flip it. Chill the crust until baking time.

Place a pie made with a pastry crust in a very hot oven and then reduce the temperature. The initial high temperature helps produce a light and flaky crust.

Spices ~

Ground spices lose their fresh flavor as they sit on a shelf. Buy nutmeg whole and grate it on a fine grater.

If you do a lot of baking, consider investing in a small electric grinder (a coffee grinder works well) and buying other spices whole (e.g. cardamon, cloves and cinnamon).

Eggs ~

These recipes use Grade A large eggs. Always bring eggs to room temperature before using, as they will blend better and beat lighter. Never add a hot ingredient to a mixture that contains eggs, as they will start to cook and will not respond properly when baked. When beating egg whites, whip them at high speed until they are stiff but not dry. Fold them into a batter gently with a rubber spatula. When adding liquid sweeteners or extracts to egg whites, beat whites until stiff, then beat in liquid at high speed. Extra unbeaten egg whites can be frozen until needed.

Nuts ~

Varieties of nuts vary in oil content as well as in flavor, and thus are not always interchangeable ; e.g. an Almond Torte can be changed to a Hazelnut Torte, but walnuts would be too oily for this recipe. Grind nuts in a nut grinder, food processor or blender. With the latter two, grind nuts at most ⅓ cup at a time or use a pulsating setting so that the nuts are ground quickly and evenly without beginning to extract the oil. Store nuts, raw or toasted, in the refrigerator or freezer to preserve freshness.

Kitchen Utensils

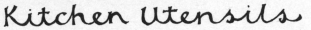

These recipes do not use any unusual or exotic kitchen tools. Gather all utensils before starting. This will save the frustration of a frantic last~minute search which could upset the careful timing of a delicate dessert.

Try to use the utensil specified. Always use a wire whisk when called for. A whisk mixes more quickly and lightly than a spoon, and also whips air into a mixture. Use the correct pan size. If the pan size must be changed, remember to adjust the baking time accordingly.

Test the oven occasionally with an oven thermometer to ensure correct baking temperatures. Also test a candy thermometer by placing it in a pan of boiling water for several minutes. It should read 212° (100° c.). For accuracy, hold a thermometer in the center of the saucepan without touching the bottom. If it is not accurate, adjust further readings to compensate.

Non~Dairy Desserts

Preparing desserts without dairy products and eggs adds an extra challenge. Non~dairy desserts can be rich and delicious, though some~

19

times slightly heavier and moister than their dairy counterparts. Fruit juices can replace milk or yogurt in many recipes, as can nut milk, a rich frothy liquid made by whipping cashews or sunflower seeds with water in a blender or food processor. Use nut milks strained or un~strained. Substitute a nut butter such as peanut butter or tahini for butter. Or, if melted butter is called for, use a light-flavored oil. Tofu takes the place of eggs in many non~dairy desserts. It adds a lightness and also helps in bind~ing. Crumble tofu into a blender or food processor. Add about ¼ c. liquid (oil or juice) to each 6 oz. of tofu and blend until light and creamy.

muffins

Mix wet and dry muffin in~gredients separately. Oil muffin tin, and then combine ingredients with as few strokes as possible.

Bake in a preheated hot oven (350°~400°).

Muffins are done when center peaks are firm to the touch. As soon as muffins are removed from the oven, slam the tin down onto a counter several times quite hard. Muffins should then come out of tin easily. If muffins don't peak, either the batter was too runny or was mixed too much, or the oven temperature was too low.

Frosting & Decorating

Always cool a cake or torte completely be~ fore removing from pans to frost. Most frosting should be chilled to obtain the proper spread~ ing consistency: neither runny, nor hard and stiff. A very thick frosting may need to stand at room temperature briefly before spreading. If a cake is crumbly, cover it with a thin layer of frosting and chill to catch the crumbs. Then the rest of the frost~ ing can be spread crumb~free over it. If crumbs do show through a frosting, hide them with a light sprinkling of chopped nuts or grated chocolate (chill chocolate for easier grating).

Decorate cakes and tortes with freshly~ picked flowers, fresh fruit or whole shelled nuts. Choose flowers that are edible, like violets, or those that last well out of water. Cut stems to $1\frac{1}{2}'' \sim 2''$ and press them lightly into frosting. Overlap flowers so the stems are hidden. Choose fruits that do not dis~ color quickly for decorating, or soak them (apples, bananas, peaches) in lemon juice to help preserve color. A ring of fresh berries around the top edge of a cake makes a simple yet attractive border, as do walnut halves or whole almonds laid side by side.

using a Pastry Bag

Decorating a cake or pie with a pastry bag adds an extra flourish; while not essential, it is fun and, with a little practise, fairly easy. Besides being decorative, an edge of rosettes can hide an uneven edge of frosting, a seam between a glaze or a fruit topping and a frosting, or a slight lopsidedness of a cake. A small starred opening is best for making rosettes. For lettering, a very small round opening is easiest.

Prepare a small amount of frosting of thicker consistency than for spreading. Add non~instant dry milk powder to Cream Cheese Frosting to stiffen. Make frosting a contrasting color for lettering: a bit of cocoa or carob powder will darken white frosting. Beet juice will produce a light pink or a deep red color.

Start with chilled frosting. Insert tip in pastry bag and fill halfway with frosting. Fold the top and squeeze until the frosting begins to pass through the tip and all the air in the bag has escaped. Practice for a moment on a plate before decorating the cake or pie. Place rosettes on the top of a cake, not on the sides where they can slip. If sprinkling frosted cake or pie with nuts or chocolate, do this before decorating, so that decorations stand out above the sprinkled surface.

Converting Recipes

There is an art to converting white flour ~ white sugar recipes to recipes using whole foods. Exact substitutions won't work because the two sets of ingredients have quite different qualities from one another. Understanding these differences will lead to success.

When reworking a recipe, don't attempt to create a carbon copy of an old favorite. Rather, aim at creating a new version which incorporates the special qualities of whole grains and natural sweeteners. Both add their own subtle flavors to desserts. Whole grains produce a slightly heavier texture than refined flour, and most natural sweeteners are liquid.

Exchanging a liquid sweetener such as honey or maple syrup for dry sugar changes the balance of dry to wet ingredients in a recipe. In a few instances this will not upset the final product. In most desserts, other changes must be made to compensate.

In general, replace each cup of sugar with ½ ~ ⅔ cup of liquid natural sweetener. Reduce other liquids in the recipe by the same amount, and slightly increase the amount of dry ingredients. Add extra flour or experiment with adding other flavors and textures such as cocoa, carob powder, wheat germ or finely ~ ground nuts. Increase a thickening agent slightly to compensate for added liquid in a recipe.

Replace sugar syrups with an equal amount of liquid natural sweeteners. Candy thermometer temperatures remain the same. One tablespoon of blackstrap molasses added to ½ cup of maple syrup or barley malt syrup creates a butterscotch flavor surprisingly like that derived from white sugar.

Many standard recipes call for creaming butter and sugar together. First cream the butter thoroughly and then beat in the liquid sweetener. Similarly, whip a liquid sweetener into egg whites or whipping cream that are already beaten stiff. The sweetener must be at room temperature to be incorporated properly into butter and egg whites.

Eggs will help in binding a mixture that would otherwise be too runny. Certain fresh fruit pies and cheesecakes may not set properly when made with a liquid sweetener. Increasing the eggs, or turning a filling into a custard, as in our Peach Custard Pie, is one solution.

Several simple tricks help compensate for the heavier texture of whole grains. Increase the baking powder or other leavening agent. Sift and even double-sift the flour to make it lighter. Add an extra egg or egg white to a recipe. Beat the whites separately and fold them into a batter at the last minute. The air incorporated into the expanded egg white will yield a light, airy cake or torte.

With proper handling (see Baking Hints, pages 15~16), we find that almost all fine pastry baking can be done with natural foods.

There are very few desserts that can not be improved with whole foods. Without sacrificing quality or flavor, this will help meet today's increasing demand for more healthful eating.

Tortes,
Cakes,
Cheesecakes
and
Cobblers

ALMOND torte

12~16 servings ~ preheat oven to 350°; lightly oil the bottoms only of 3 9" round layer pans; prep. 1 hr. ; baking 25 min. + 20~30 min.; cooling 30 min.

- 2 c. almonds, whole
- 1¼ c. sifted whole wheat pastry flour
- 1½ t. baking powder

- 3 T. butter
- 6 eggs, separated
- 1 c. maple syrup
- ½ t. vanilla extract
- ½ t. almond extract
- ¼ c. orange juice

> The secret of a light torte is in the thorough beating of the egg yolks. They are beaten far longer than the whites.

★ Start with all ingredients at room temperature.

★ Toast the almonds in a 350° oven for 25 min~ utes, stirring occasionally. Then grind them finely in a grinder or blender. Measure out 1½ c. ground almonds (firmly packed). Reduce oven temperature to 325°.

★ Sift flour, separating out and discarding the coarsest bran; measure after sifting.

★ Mix measured almonds with sifted flour and baking powder.

★ Melt butter and set it aside to cool.

★ Beat egg yolks for 6 minutes with an electric mixer on high speed.

★ Add in ⅓ c. of the maple syrup and beat for 3 more minutes; repeat process with each remaining ⅓ c. of syrup.

★ Beat in vanilla and almond extracts.

· Continued on next page.

★ Continue beating until yolks are very creamy and will thickly coat a spoon. They will have increased in volume about 5 times. This will take a total of 15~20 minutes beating time.

★ Then briefly beat in cooled butter and orange juice.

★ Fold dry ingredients into the yolk mixture with a rubber spatula.

★ Beat egg whites until stiff but not dry, and gently fold into batter.

★ Pour batter into prepared pans and bake for 20~30 minutes at 325°. Torte is done when a toothpick inserted in the center comes out clean.

★ Cool layers in pans.

★ Frost cooled torte and sprinkle remaining ground almonds on top.

★ See Torte Frosting Suggestions, page 31.

TORTES

Chocolate Almond ★ Chocolate Mint

★ Follow recipe for Almond Torte, page 28.

★ Increase **baking powder** to **2t.**

★ Increase **butter** to ¼ c.

★ Add ⅓ c. **honey** along with the **maple syrup.**

★ Add ½ c. **unsweetened cocoa** to the dry ingredients.

★ Follow recipe for Chocolate Almond Torte, this page.

★ Substitute ¼ t. **pure mint extract** for almond extract.

★ Substitute ¼ c. **strong mint tea** for orange juice.

★ Frost with Whipped Cream Frosting, page 150, adding a drop of **mint extract** to whipping cream, if desired.

★ Decorate with fresh mint leaves.

Torte frosting suggestions

★ Layer and frost with **Whipped Cream Frosting**, page 150. ★ Layer with **Marzipan Filling**, page 152, and frost with **Whipped Cream Frosting**, page 150. ★ Layer with **raspberry preserves** (honey-sweetened, if available), and frost with **Whipped Cream Frosting**, page 150. ★ Layer with **Whipped Cream Frosting**, page 150. Cover top with 1½ c. fresh, very dry **blueberries** in an even layer. Prepare ½ c. **Honey Glaze**, page 155, and pour it over berries while hot. Berries must be dry or the glaze will run off. Frost sides of torte with **Whipped Cream Frosting**.

Peach or Strawberry Shortcake

· Almond Torte, page 28
· 9 large, ripe peaches **or** 4 pints fresh strawberries
· ⅓ c. maple syrup (optional)
· 1 c. heavy cream

★ Prepare Almond Torte as directed. Cool completely.

★ For **Peach Shortcake** : Skin peaches by dropping them a few at a time into a sauce-pan of boiling water. Cook for two minutes, then plunge them into a bowl of ice water. The loosened skin will pull right off. Slice peaches thinly and mix with maple syrup. Let fruit sit for at least 15 minutes. Set some aside for topping.

★ For **Strawberry Shortcake** : Slice 3 pints of the berries and mix with maple syrup. Leave remaining pint whole.

★ Generously layer torte with fruit just before serving.
★ Top with whipped cream.
★ Decorate with remaining peach slices or remaining whole berries.

mm

Neapolitan Torte

14~16 servings ~ preheat oven to 325°; lightly oil the bottoms only of 3 9" round pans; prep. 1¼ hrs.; baking 20~30 min.; cooling 30 min.

A few extra steps and a few more mixing bowls turn the Almond Torte into a striking, striped torte that will baffle its admirers.

- ½ c. finely ground toasted almonds, firmly packed
- 1¼ c. whole wheat pastry flour, sifted and then measured
- 2 t. baking powder
- ⅓ c. unsweetened cocoa

- 4 T. butter
- 6 eggs, separated
- 1 c. maple syrup
- ¼ c. honey
- ½ t. vanilla extract
- ½ t. almond extract
- ¼ c. orange juice

★ Before starting, read the directions for handling egg yolks in recipe for Almond Torte, pages 28~29.
★ Mix almonds, flour and baking powder together. Separate out 1 c., then add cocoa to remaining dry mix.
★ Melt butter; set aside to cool.
★ Beat egg yolks 6 minutes. Gradually beat in syrup, honey and extracts; beat 15~20 minutes in all. Then beat in cooled butter and orange juice.
★ Fold 1¾ c. of whipped yolks into the 1 c. of plain dry mix.
★ Fold remaining yolks into dry cocoa mix.
★ Beat egg whites until stiff but not dry. Fold ⅔ of them (estimate, don't measure!) into chocolate batter and ⅓ into plain batter.
★ Spread chocolate batter into 2 oiled pans; plain batter into third.
★ Bake for 20~30 minutes until a toothpick inserted in the center of pan comes out clean.
★ Layer the cooled torte with plain layer between the two chocolate layers.
★ See Torte Frosting Suggestions, page 31.

MF

danish cardamon
~CAKE~

~a light tea cake with the surprising flavor of an unusual spice~

8~10 servings ~ preheat oven to 325°; lightly oil the bottoms only of 2 8" round layer pans; prep. 1 hr. ; baking 15~20 min. ; cooling 30 min.

- ¾ c. hazelnuts, finely ground and firmly packed
- ½ c. + 2 T. whole wheat pastry flour
- 1 t. baking powder
- 1 t. cardamon, freshly-ground
  (or 1½ ~ 2 t. pre-ground)

- ¼ c. butter
- 3 eggs, separated
- ¼ c. maple syrup
- ¼ c. honey
- ½ t. vanilla extract
- ⅓ recipe Cream Cheese Frosting, page 148

★ Before starting, read the directions for beating egg yolks in the Almond Torte recipe, pages 28~29.

★ Mix dry ingredients together.

★ Melt butter. Set aside to cool.

★ Beat egg yolks. Beat in sweeteners and vanilla extract. Beat 15~20 minutes.

★ Beat in cooled butter, then fold whipped yolks into dry ingredients.

★ Beat egg whites to soft peaks and gently fold into batter.

★ Pour batter into prepared pans and bake for 15~20 minutes. Cakes are done when a tooth~pick inserted in the center comes out clean.

★ Prepare frosting, adding a pinch of cardamon if desired.

★ Cool layers completely in pans before frosting.

Black Forest C★A★K★E

14 servings ~ preheat oven to 325°;
3 oiled 9" round layer pans;
prep. 2 hr.; baking 20-30 min.;
cooling 30 min.

- Chocolate Almond Torte, page 30
- 1½ lbs. fresh sweet cherries, pitted
- Semi-Sweet Chocolate Glaze, page 154
- Whipped Cream Frosting, page 150, substituting 1 T. cherry brandy for vanilla extract

★ Prepare torte as directed, substituting **hazelnuts** for almonds and substituting 2 T. **cherry brandy** for vanilla and almond extracts.

★ Cool baked cake.

★ Prepare chocolate glaze.

★ Measure out 2 c. whole cherries. Pit and chop them. Drain cherries well and mix with hot chocolate glaze. Spread glaze on first two layers of torte.

★ Frost with Whipped Cream Frosting.

★ Slice remaining cherries in half, discard pits and place cherries cut side down over the top of the torte.

★ If fresh cherries are not available, layer with plain chocolate glaze. Frost sides with Whipped Cream Frosting and spread top with Cherry Topping, page 156, using canned cherries.

mm

Cherry Walnut torte

12 servings ~ preheat oven to 350°; lightly oil the bottom only of 1 9" round pan; prep. 1¾ hr.; baking 25 min.; cooling 30 min.

- 4 eggs, separated
- 2 c. walnuts, finely ground
- ⅜ c. maple syrup
- 1 t. vanilla extract or Kirsch
- Cherry Topping, page 156
- ½ c. heavy cream (optional)

This traditional torte contains no flour.

★ Beat egg yolks with an electric beater for 5 minutes.

★ While eggs are beating, grind walnuts. Measure them ground but not packed down.

★ Add syrup and vanilla to yolks and continue beating 5 more minutes.

★ Gently fold nuts into yolks with a rubber spatula.

★ Beat egg whites until soft peaks form, then fold them into batter.

★ Pour into oiled cake pan and bake at 350° for 10 minutes. Reduce heat to 325° and bake an additional 10~15 minutes until a toothpick inserted in the center of the torte comes out dry. Cool torte before removing from pan.

★ Prepare Cherry Topping.

★ Turn torte onto a serving platter. Spread with cooled topping.

★ Whip cream until stiff.

★ Using a pastry bag, make a rim of rosettes with the cream around the top edge of the torte. See page 22 for decorating hints.

Poppy Seed Torte

- ⅔ c. poppy seeds
- ⅔ c. milk
- ⅔ c. maple syrup
- ¼ c. honey
- 2 t. vanilla extract
- ⅓ c. butter
- ⅓ c. oil
- 4 eggs, separated, plus 2 extra whites

- 2 c. whole wheat pastry flour, sifted and then measured
- 5 t. baking powder

★ Soak poppy seeds in milk, sweeteners and vanilla extract for one hour.

★ Melt butter, then add oil to cool the butter quickly.

★ Beat egg yolks for two minutes; then beat in cooled butter.

★ Mix flour and baking powder together.

★ Combine all wet ingredients and beat into dry ingredients.

★ Beat egg whites until stiff but not dry, and gently fold them into batter with a rubber spatula.

★ Pour batter into prepared pans and bake for 25 minutes, until a toothpick inserted in the center of torte comes out clean.

★ Frost cooled torte with Cream Cheese Frosting, page 148, or follow the suggestions on page 37.

Poppy Seed Torte with Egg Custard Filling

9 servings ~ 1 oiled 9"x 9"x 2" square baking pan; prep. 1½ hr.

· Egg Custard Filling, page 151
· Poppy Seed Torte, page 36

★ Prepare Egg Custard Filling and chill.

★ Prepare Poppy Seed Torte as directed. Bake in 1 9"x 9" pan, instead of 3 layer pans, for 40 minutes, until center of cake is firm. Cool in pan.

★ Cut cake into 9 pieces. Slice each piece in thirds, horizontally.

★ Spoon two heaping tablespoons of custard on first two layers and stack all three layers on top of each other on a dessert dish. Custard will spill over the edges and gracefully fall to the plate. Cake must be cut into individual servings before layering with custard. Cutting it afterwards causes all the filling to ooze out.

Glazed Poppy Seed Torte

10 servings ~ 3 8" round cake pans, oiled; prep. 1½ hr.

· Poppy Seed Torte, page 36
· 3 oz. raspberry jam, honey~sweetened if available
· Semi~Sweet Chocolate Glaze, page 154
OR
· Raspberry Glaze, page 155
· ½ recipe Cream Cheese Frosting, page 148

★ Prepare torte as directed.

★ Layer cooled torte with raspberry jam.

★ Prepare Chocolate Glaze or Raspberry Glaze and top torte while glaze is still hot.

★ Frost sides with Cream Cheese Frosting.

★ Using a pastry bag, make a round of rosettes to hide the seam between chocolate and cream cheese (optional). See page 22 for decorating hints.

★ Chill torte until ready to serve.

Dark Chocolate CAKE

16 servings ~ preheat oven to 325°; 3 oiled 9" round cake pans; prep. 1¼ hr.; baking 20~30 min.; cooling 40 min.

- 4 oz. unsweetened chocolate
- ⅓ c. strong coffee
- ⅓ c. milk
- ¾ c. butter
- 1 c. maple syrup
  - ¾ c. honey
  - 4 eggs, separated
  - 4 t. vanilla extract
  - ¼ c. orange juice

- 2¼ c. whole wheat pastry flour, sifted
- 1 T. baking powder

★ Start with all ingredients at room temperature.

★ Melt chocolate in a double boiler, remove from heat and stir in coffee and milk.

★ Cream butter until smooth. Beat in sweeteners.

★ Slowly beat in egg yolks, vanilla, orange juice and cooled chocolate mixture. Beat just until well-blended.

★ Sift pastry flour, separating out and discarding the largest flecks of bran. Measure the flour after sifting.

★ Mix flour and baking powder and briefly beat into chocolate batter.

★ Beat egg whites until they form soft peaks but are not dry. Fold whites into the batter.

★ Pour batter into oiled pans.

★ Bake for 20~30 minutes. A toothpick inserted in the center should come out nearly clean.

★ The best chocolate cakes are taken out a bit underdone. They continue to bake as they cool. They will stay fresh longer if they are slightly fudge~like in texture.

★ Cool layers completely in their pans.

★ Layer and frost with Chocolate Cream Cheese Frosting, page 149, Whipped Cream Frosting, page 150, or Green Mountain Frosting, page 147.

DUTCH CHOCOLATE Cake

16 servings ~ preheat oven to 325°;
3 oiled 9" round cake pans;
prep. 1¼ hr.; baking 30 min.; cooling 30 min.

· 3 oz. unsweetened chocolate
· ⅔ c. milk
· ¾ c. butter
· ¾ c. maple syrup
· ¾ c. honey
· 4 eggs, separated
· 1 t. vanilla extract
· ½ t. pure orange or lemon extract
· 1 t. grated orange peel
· ½ c. frozen orange juice concentrate (at room temperature)
· 2¼ c whole wheat pastry flour
· 1 T. baking powder
· Chocolate Cream Cheese Frosting, page 149

* Melt chocolate in a double boiler. Add milk and cool.
* Cream butter, then beat in maple syrup and honey.
* Gradually beat in egg yolks, extracts, orange peel and orange juice concentrate.
* Sift pastry flour to separate out largest flecks of bran. Measure after sifting.
* Mix flour and baking powder and beat into batter.
* Beat egg whites to soft peaks and fold into batter.
* Pour batter into oiled pans and bake for 20~30 minutes until toothpick inserted into center of cake comes out clean.
* Prepare frosting. Add a few drops of pure orange extract if desired.
* Layer and frost cooled cake.

German Chocolate Cake

* Prepare and bake Dark Chocolate Cake, page 38.

* Layer and frost with German Coconut Frosting, page 146.

mm

Chocolate Strawberry Cake

14~16 servings ~ preheat oven to 325°;
3 oiled 9" round cake pans;
prep 1¾ hr.; baking 20~30 min.;
cooling 40 min.

· 1 Dark Chocolate Cake, page 38
· ½ recipe Semi~Sweet Chocolate Glaze, page 154
· 1 pint fresh strawberries
· 4 oz. strawberry jam (honey~ sweetened if available)
· Whipped Cream Frosting, page 150.

★ Prepare Dark Chocolate Cake as directed. Substitute a fruity liqueur for the vanilla extract, if desired.

★ Prepare glaze.

★ Wash strawberries and pat them dry with paper towels. Leave berries whole and do not remove green tops.

★ Dip berries in hot glaze, leaving the top third of each one unglazed. Set upside down on waxed paper to harden, and refrigerate until cake is frosted.

★ Layer cooled cake with strawberry jam.

★ Frost with Whipped Cream Frosting.

★ Arrange the glazed berries on top of the frosted cake and around the bottom.

MF

German Carob Cake

10~12 servings ~ preheat oven to 350°;
3 oiled 8" round cake pans;
prep. 1 hr.; baking 15~20 min.; cooling 30 min.

- 2 c. whole wheat pastry flour
- ⅔ c. carob powder
- 2 t. baking powder

- 1 c. butter
- ½ c. maple syrup
- ½ c. honey
- 6 eggs, separated
- ⅓ c. plain yogurt
- 2 t. vanilla extract
- German Coconut Frosting, page 146

~ a variation on the traditional German Chocolate Cake ~

★ Sift dry ingredients together.
★ Melt butter and mix with sweeteners.
★ Beat egg yolks for 5 minutes with an electric mixer on high speed.
★ Add yogurt and vanilla and beat 5 more minutes.
★ Beat in cooled butter mixture.
★ Combine wet and dry ingredients and beat until smooth.
★ Whip egg whites to soft peaks and fold them into the batter.
★ Pour batter into oiled cake pans.
★ Bake for 15~20 minutes until a toothpick inserted in the center comes out dry.
★ Cool layers completely in their pans.
★ Layer and frost with German Coconut Frosting.

mf

carob rum ice cream cake

- 1¾ c. whole wheat pastry flour
- 1 c. carob powder
- 5 t. baking powder
- 2 t. cinnamon
- 1 t. ground cloves

- ½ c. butter
- ½ c. maple syrup
- ¼ c. honey
- 5 eggs, separated
- 1 t. vanilla extract
- 1 c. milk

- ½ c. rum (or fruit juice)
- ½ gallon vanilla or honey ice cream
  ¾ c. toasted almond slivers

12~16 servings ~ preheat oven to 350°;
2 oiled 9" round cake pans;
prep 1½ hr.; baking 20~25 min.; cooling/freezing 3½ hr.

★ Start with all cake ingredients at room temperature.
★ Sift flour and carob powder and mix with other dry ingredients.
★ Cream butter, then add sweeteners and beat until smooth.
★ Beat in egg yolks and vanilla.
★ Alternately beat in dry ingredients and milk to the butter mixture until all is combined and smooth.
★ Whip egg whites until stiff but not dry and fold into batter.
★ Pour into oiled pans and bake for 20~25 minutes. Cake is done when a toothpick inserted in the center comes out dry.
★ Cool layers completely before proceeding.

· Continued on next page.

★ It's best not to layer the cake in the heat of a summer day. Even on a cool evening work quickly or the ice cream will run away from you ~ leaving you with ice cream soup.

★ Clear a space in freezer for cake before getting started.

★ Cut both cake layers in half horizontally, four layers in all.

★ Sprinkle rum or juice on each layer. Refrigerate layers until ready to frost each one.

★ Soften your favorite vanilla ice cream until it is easy to spread, but is not melting (or use fresh homemade ice cream which is usually softer than store-bought).

★ Spread ice cream on top of first layer and place in freezer. Spread next layer and place on top of first. Continue process with remaining layers. Spread top layer especially thick, then garnish with almonds while ice cream is still soft.

★ Freeze layered cake for 1½ hours until ice cream is solid and layers don't slide around.

★ Then frost sides with remaining ice cream.

★ Freeze at least one more hour before serving.

Carrot cake

16~20 servings ~ preheat oven to 350°;
3 oiled 9" round cake pans or 1 oiled 11"x 17" baking pan;
prep. 1 hr.; baking 25~30 min.; cooling 45 min.

- 3½ c. grated carrots, tightly packed
- (3-4 large carrots)
- 1 c. maple syrup
- ⅔ c. honey
- 2 T. blackstrap molasses
- 2 t. cinnamon
- ¼ t. powdered ginger
- ¼ t. ground cardamon
- pinch each of grated nutmeg, allspice and mace.

- 1 c. butter
- 6 eggs, separated
- juice of ½ lemon (about 2 T.)
- ½ t. vanilla extract
- ½ c. orange juice

- 4 c. whole wheat pastry flour, sifted
- 1 T. baking powder
- ½ c. raisins
- ½ c. walnuts, finely chopped
- Cream Cheese Frosting, page 148

★ Start with all ingredients at room temperature.

★ Cook grated carrots in a saucepan over medium heat with sweeteners and all the spices for 10 minutes. Stir occasionally and reduce heat if mixture begins to boil. Cool.

★ Cream butter and egg yolks until smooth.

★ Beat in lemon juice, vanilla and orange juice.

★ Add cooled carrot mixture.

★ Sift flour, separating out the coarsest bran flakes. Measure flour after sifting.

★ Mix flour and baking powder and beat into batter.

★ Stir in raisins and half the walnuts.

★ Beat egg whites until they are stiff but not dry and fold them into the batter.

★ Pour batter into oiled layer pans and bake for 20~25 minutes (25~30 minutes for large flat pan), until a toothpick inserted in the center of cake comes out clean.

★ Cool layers in pans.

★ Prepare Cream Cheese Frosting and frost cooled cake. Sprinkle remaining walnuts on top.

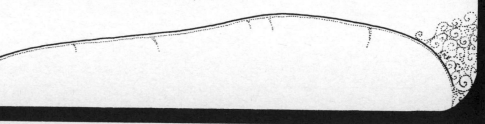

mm

APPLE CAKE

15 servings ~ preheat oven to 350°;
1 oiled 9"x13" cake pan or 2 oiled 9" round cake pans;
prep. 1 hr.; baking 30~40 min.; cooling 45 min.

- 2⅓ c. peeled, grated baking apples, measured packed (4 medium apples)
- ⅔ c. butter
- 4 eggs, separated
- ⅔ c. maple syrup
- ⅓ c. honey
- ¼ c. yogurt
- ½ t. vanilla extract
- juice and grated rind of ½ lemon

- 2⅔ c. sifted whole wheat pastry flour
- 2 t. baking powder
- 1¾ t. cinnamon
- ⅛ t. each of ginger, cardamon, nutmeg, allspice and mace
- ½ c. walnuts, chopped
- Cream Cheese Frosting, page 148; ½ recipe for 9"x13" cake, full recipe for 9" layer cake.

★ Start with ingredients at room temperature.
★ Peel, core and grate apples.
★ Cream butter until smooth.
★ Beat in egg yolks.
★ Beat in syrup, honey, yogurt, vanilla, lemon juice and grated lemon rind.
★ Stir in grated apples.
★ In a separate bowl, mix dry ingredients together.
★ Stir dry ingredients into wet ingredients. Add half the walnuts.
★ Beat egg whites to soft peaks and fold into batter.
★ Pour batter into oiled pan(s) and bake for 30~40 minutes, until a toothpick inserted in the center comes out dry.
★ Cool cake in pan(s).
★ (Layer and) frost with Cream Cheese Frosting, and sprinkle remaining walnuts on top.

Banana Cake ~ a heavy, moist cake. For a lighter cake, reduce the **bananas** to 1¾ c.

★ Follow recipe for Apple Cake, this page. ★ substitute 2⅓ c. mashed bananas (5 medium bananas) for the apples. ★ Omit cinnamon, ginger, allspice and mace. ★ Increase grated **nutmeg** to ½ t., **cardamon** to ½ t. if freshly-ground, 1 t. if pre-ground. ★ Frost with **Cream Cheese** or **Chocolate Cream Cheese Frosting**, pages 148~49.

MF

holiday fruitcake

· 5 c. (1½ lbs.) of mixed dried fruits
  and nuts :
    1½ c. currants
    ⅔ c. sunflower seeds
    ⅔ c. walnuts, chopped
    1 c. date pieces
    ½ c. dried apples, chopped
    ⅓ c. raisins
    ⅓ c. figs, chopped

· 1 c. + 2 T. whole wheat pastry flour
· ½ c. butter
· ¼ c. honey
· 1 T. molasses
· 3 eggs
· ¼ t. baking powder
· ¼ t. baking soda
· ¼ t. salt
· ½ t. each of cinnamon, allspice,
  ginger and cloves
· brandy, rum or fruit juice *

2 8"x 4" loaves or 1 9"x 5" loaf ;
preheat oven to 275° ;
prep. 45 min. ; baking 2 hr. ; aging 1~2 months
                                    (optional)

Fruitcake is more fruit and nuts than
cake. The dried fruit, nut and seed mix
listed is just one of many possibilities.
Vary the mix to suit your taste and
budget.

★ Start with all ingredients at room
  temperature.

★ Mix dried fruits and nuts together,
  and dredge in 2 T. flour.

★ Cream butter in a mixer, then beat
  in honey, molasses and eggs.

★ Mix remaining 1 c. flour with other
  dry ingredients, then beat into the
  butter.

★ Stir dry fruit mix into batter.

★ Line loaf pans with brown paper (paper bags work well) or foil, leaving enough extra to cover the top so cakes can be completely wrapped as they bake.

★ Spread batter into pans, wrap and bake at 275° for 2 hours.

★ Place a baking pan filled with 3 cups of hot water on the floor of the oven while cakes are baking. This will keep cakes from drying out. Cool cakes in their pans.

* Traditionally, fruitcake is made at least one month early and soaked in brandy or rum to age. Wrap cakes in liquor~soaked cheesecloth and refrigerate in a closed container. Check cloth weekly and resoak it if it begins to dry out.

  For a non~alcoholic fruitcake, soak cheesecloth in fruit juice instead. A juice~soaked cake will not keep for as long, however, as juice will not preserve the cake the same way alcohol will.

Pumpkin Cheesecake

10~12 servings ~ preheat oven to 375°;
1 10" springform pan;
prep. 45 min.; baking 1¾ hr.;
cooling/setting 2 hr. ~ overnight.

- 1 Graham Cracker Cheesecake Crust, page 120
- 1 very small fresh pumpkin
- 1¼ lbs. cream cheese, softened
- 1½ c. maple syrup
- 1 egg
- ½ c. whipping cream
- 1 t. blackstrap molasses
- 2 T. arrowroot
- 1 T. vanilla extract
- ½ t. cinnamon
- ½ t. powdered ginger
- pinch each of ground cloves, allspice and nutmeg

★ Prepare crust and prebake it for 5 minutes at 375°.

★ Cut pumpkin in half and set it in a baking pan, cut sides down. Fill pan with ½ inch of water. Bake for 45 minutes, until very soft. Peel skin away and measure out 1¾ c. pulp. Freeze extra pumpkin for another cheesecake or pie.

★ Beat cream cheese until smooth.

★ In a blender or food processor, purée measured pumpkin with maple syrup.

★ Whip all ingredients together until creamy.

★ Pour filling evenly over crust and bake at 375° for about 1 hour. Cake is done even if center is not completely set.

★ Allow cheesecake to cool and set completely before cutting, at least 2 hours. Best if refrigerated overnight.

48

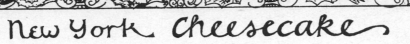

New York Cheesecake

12 servings ~ preheat oven to 375°;
1 10" springform pan;
prep. 30 min.; baking 1 hr.; cooling/setting
2 hr. ~ overnight

· 1 Graham Cracker Cheesecake
   Crust, page 120
· 2 lbs. cream cheese, softened
· 1 c. maple syrup
· 1½ t. vanilla extract
· ½ c. whipping cream
· 1 egg
· 2 T. arrowroot

★ Prepare crust and prebake it for
   5 minutes at 375°.
★ Beat cream cheese.
★ Add all ingredients and whip until
   creamy in a blender, food processor
   or mixer set on high speed.
★ Spread mixture evenly over crust
   and bake at 375° for 45 minutes to
   1 hour. Cheesecake may not have
set completely in center, but if mostly firm it's done. Cool for at least 2
hours before cutting. Cheesecake is best if allowed to set overnight.
★ Serve plain, or topped with fresh fruit, a fruit topping, or a fruit or
chocolate glaze.

Marbled Cheesecake

· New York Cheesecake, this page
· 2 oz. unsweetened chocolate
· ½ c. maple syrup.

★ Prepare cheesecake filling and pour
   into crust. ★ Melt chocolate in a
   double boiler and add maple syrup.
★ Cool chocolate syrup for 15 minutes,
   then swirl it through the cheesecake
filling just enough to get a marbled effect.   ★ Bake as directed above.

Yogurt cheesecake

~a light, tangy cheesecake~

12 servings ~ preheat oven to 350°;
1 10" springform pan;
prep. 1 hr.; baking 1 hr.; cooling/setting 2 hr.

- 1 Graham Cracker Cheesecake Crust, page 120
- 3 c. plain yogurt
- 1 c. cream cheese
- ½ c. sour cream
- ¾ c. maple syrup
- 4 eggs, separated
- 2 t. Amaretto (almond liqueur)
- ½ t. vanilla extract
- 2 T. arrowroot mixed with 2 T. water

★ Prepare crumb crust and prebake it for 5 minutes at 350°.

★ Drain yogurt through 4 layers of cheesecloth suspended over a bowl for about 30 minutes, until ¾ c. of clear liquid has drained out, leaving 2 c. of thick yogurt. The kitchen faucet is a good place to suspend cheese~ cloth from. Save the drained liquid for a healthy drink or for soup stock.

★ Whip yogurt, cream cheese and sour cream in a blender or food processor until smooth.

★ Blend in maple syrup.

★ Lightly beat egg yolks and add to mixture.

★ Stir in Amaretto, vanilla extract and arrowroot.

★ Beat two egg whites to soft peaks and gently fold them into the filling with a rubber spatula.

★ Pour filling into crust and bake for 50~60 minutes until set. Cake is set when center is firm.

★ Cool completely before cutting.

MF

ricotta walnut cheesecake

12 servings ~ preheat oven to 350°;
1 10" springform pan ;

prep. 30 min.; baking 1 hr.;
cooling 1½ hr.

- 1 Graham Cracker Cheesecake Crust, page 120
- 1½ lbs. ricotta cheese
- ½ c. maple syrup
- ¼ c. honey
- 5 eggs
- 2 t. vanilla extract
- 1 T. lemon juice
- 1 T. arrowroot
- pinch salt
- ⅜ c. chopped walnuts

* Prepare crust.

* In a blender or food processor, whip cheese with syrup and honey until smooth.

* Continue blending and add eggs, vanilla, lemon juice, arrowroot and salt.

* Stir in nuts.

* Pour over crust and bake for 45~60 minutes until set. Cake is set when center is firm.

* Serve plain or top with fresh fruit or a fruit topping.

MF

BLUEBERRY cobbler

9 servings ~ preheat oven to 350°;
1 oiled 9"x9" pan ;
prep. 45 min.; baking 30~35 min.

- 1¾ c. whole wheat pastry flour
- 1 T. baking powder
- ½ t. salt

- 1 c. milk
- 3 T. oil
- 1 c. honey
- 2 c. fresh blueberries (or frozen unsweetened berries)
- ⅓ c. water
- 1 T. arrowroot mixed with 2 T. water

★ Mix dry ingredients together.

★ Mix milk, oil and ⅔ c. of the honey in a second bowl.

★ In a saucepan bring blueberries, water and remaining ⅓ c. honey to a gentle boil. Stir arrowroot mixture and add. Stir constantly with a wire whisk until juice thickens. Then remove from heat.

★ Combine dry and wet cake ingredients and pour into oiled pan.

★ Slowly pour hot fruit over batter. Do not stir.

★ Bake for 30~35 minutes.

PEACH cobbler

★ Follow Blueberry Cobbler recipe.

★ Substitute **7~10 large ripe peaches** for the blueberries. Peel and slice half the peaches.

★ Purée the others in a blender or food processor with the water. Combine all the peaches in a saucepan and bring to a boil. Then whisk in the arrowroot and continue cooking until fruit thickens.

mm

Raspberry Lattice Tarts

16 3½" tarts ~
preheat oven to
350°;
prep. 1½ hr.;
baking 15 min.;
chilling 3 hr.

- 1½ c. whole wheat pastry flour, sifted and then measured
- 1¼ c. almonds, finely ground and firmly packed
- ½ t. cinnamon
- ⅛ t. each of ground ginger, ground cloves and mace

- ½ c. butter
- ¼ c. maple syrup
- ¼ c. honey
- ½ t. grated lemon rind
- 2 hard-boiled egg yolks
- 1 egg yolk, raw
- 1 t. vanilla extract
- 8 oz. raspberry preserves, honey-sweetened if available

Glaze:
- 1 egg white
- 1 T. cream

★ Start with all ingredients at room temperature.

★ Mix pastry flour, almonds and spices together.

★ In a second bowl cream butter, then beat in sweeteners until smooth.

★ Beat in lemon rind, cooked and raw yolks, and vanilla.

★ Mix in dry ingredients until well-blended.

★ Refrigerate for 2~3 hours or overnight.

★ Handling as little as possible, take a portion of the dough and roll it out on a floured surface to ⅛" thick. Keep unused dough refrigerated, as it will handle best when cold.

★ Cut out 16 3½" round cookies and place them on an oiled cookie sheet. A standard sized mason jar lid makes a perfect cookie cutter.

★ Spread 2 t. preserves on each cookie.

★ To make the lattice top, cut thin (⅛" wide) strips from the dough. Roll out only small amounts of the remaining dough at a time, as the strips become unmanageable when they become too warm.

Continued on next page.

* Make a false lattice rather than actually weaving the strips : Place 4 parallel strips on a cookie; then lay 4 strips going the opposite way. Transport strips from counter to cookie on the side of a knife to keep them from breaking.

* Gently press strips down on cookies and trim any ragged edges.

* Refrigerate cookies for 10 minutes before glazing.

* With a fork, beat egg white and cream for glaze. Glaze top of tarts with a pastry brush.

* Bake on top rack of oven at 350° for 10~15 minutes until golden brown.

Peanut Butter & Jelly cookies

4½ dozen cookies ~ preheat oven to 350°; prep. 1 hr.; chilling 3 hr. ~ overnight; baking 45 min

~ a sandwich in a cookie ~

- 2 c. crunchy natural peanut butter
- 1½ c. honey
- 1 c. oil
- 2 t. vanilla extract
- 4 c. whole wheat pastry flour
- ½ c. wheat germ (optional)
- ¾ t. salt

- 4 oz. jelly or preserves, honey-sweetened if available

★ Mix wet ingredients together until completely smooth.

★ Then add the dry ingredients, stirring until they are completely incorporated into the stiff dough.

★ Refrigerate dough several hours or over-night.

★ Form balls of about 2 T. of dough and place them on an oiled cookie sheet.

★ Flatten balls lightly with a fork.

★ Then, with your thumb, make a deep impression in the center of each cookie.

★ Fill impressions with a dab of preserves.

★ Place cookie sheet on top rack of preheated oven so cookie bottoms don't become too hard.

★ Bake 8~12 minutes. Be careful not to overbake.

★ Cool cookies before removing from cookie sheet.

Raspberry Jam w/ honey

58

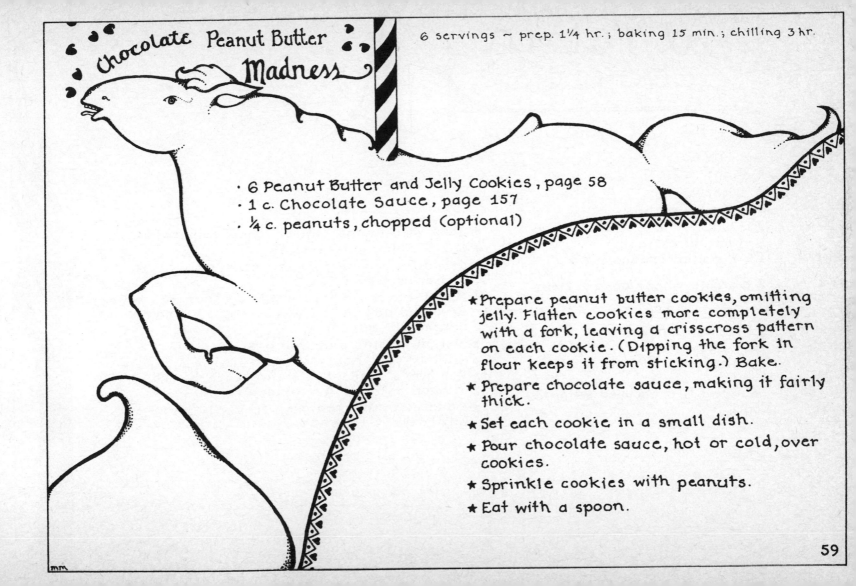

Chocolate Peanut Butter Madness

- 6 Peanut Butter and Jelly Cookies, page 58
- 1 c. Chocolate Sauce, page 157
- ¼ c. peanuts, chopped (optional)

★ Prepare peanut butter cookies, omitting jelly. Flatten cookies more completely with a fork, leaving a crisscross pattern on each cookie. (Dipping the fork in flour keeps it from sticking.) Bake.

★ Prepare chocolate sauce, making it fairly thick.

★ Set each cookie in a small dish.

★ Pour chocolate sauce, hot or cold, over cookies.

★ Sprinkle cookies with peanuts.

★ Eat with a spoon.

oatmeal raisin cookies

4 doz. large cookies ~ preheat oven to 350°; prep. 45 min.; chilling 3 hr. ~ overnight; baking 30 min.

- ½ c. butter
- 2 eggs
- ½ c. honey
- ½ c. maple syrup
- ½ c. oil
- 2 t. vanilla extract
- 1½ t. grated orange rind

- 2 c. whole wheat pastry flour
- 2 c. rolled oats
- 1 t. baking soda
- 1 t. baking powder
- ¾ t. cinnamon
- ½ t. nutmeg, freshly grated

- rounded ½ c. chopped walnuts (optional)
- rounded ½ c. raisins

★ Start with ingredients at room temperature.
★ Cream butter until smooth.
★ Gradually beat in eggs, sweeteners, oil, vanilla and orange rind.
★ Mix all the dry ingredients together in a separate bowl and add to the wet mixture, stirring until completely mixed.
★ Stir in raisins and walnuts.
★ Chill several hours or overnight.
★ Roll into 1" balls and flatten with thumb or palm of hand onto oiled cookie sheets.
★ Bake in preheated oven for 7~10 minutes until lightly browned.

Sand Tarts

·almond holiday cookies·

5 doz. 2½" round cookies ~ preheat oven to 350°; prep. 1 hr.; chilling 1 hr.; baking 30 min.

· 1 c. unsalted butter
· ¾ maple syrup
· ½ c. honey
· 1 T. vanilla extract

· 4 c. whole wheat pastry flour
· 1 c. almonds, finely ground
· pinch salt
· 1 T. cinnamon or cocoa (optional)

★ Cream butter and sweeteners.
★ Add vanilla.
★ Mix flour, almonds and salt together and stir into butter.
★ Refrigerate dough for 1 hour.
★ Roll out on a floured surface to ⅛"~¼" thick. Keep extra dough refrigerated until ready to use.
★ Cut dough with cookie cutters and sprinkle with cinnamon or cocoa.
★ Bake on oiled cookie sheets for 8~10 min~ utes, until bottoms of cookies are lightly browned.
★ Cool cookies on a rack.

mm

carob fudge nut
cookies

· ¾ c. butter
· ½ c. honey
· ⅓ c. barley malt syrup
· 3 eggs
· ½ c. crunchy, natural peanut butter
· 2 t. vanilla extract

· 1 c. whole wheat pastry flour
· 1 c. carob powder
· 1 c. rolled oats
· ¾ c. ground cashews, measured packed
· ½ c. wheat germ
· 1 T. baking powder

3 doz. large cookies ~ preheat oven to 350°; prep. 1 hr.; baking 30 min.

★ Cream butter.
★ Beat in sweeteners, eggs, peanut butter and vanilla.
★ In a second bowl combine dry ingredients.
★ Combine dry and wet ingredients and mix thoroughly.
★ Drop batter by heaping tablespoons onto an oiled cookie sheet. Leave room for expansion.
★ Flatten cookies slightly with a spoon or the palm of your hand. A wet hand will not stick to the dough.
★ Bake at 350° for 10 minutes. Remove from oven when still slightly underdone for best results.

62

MF

carob chip cookies

· ¾ c. butter
· 1 c. maple syrup
· 1 egg
· 2 t. vanilla extract

· 1¼ c. rolled oats
· 1 c. whole wheat pastry flour
· 1 c. raw wheat germ
· ½ t. salt
· 1 t. cinnamon

· ¼ c. walnuts, chopped
· ½ c. unsweetened carob chips

★ Start with ingre-dients at room temper-ature.
★ Cream the butter.
★ Slowly beat in syrup, egg and va-nilla.
★ Mix dry ingredients in a separate bowl, then stir into butter.
★ Stir in carob chips and walnuts.
★ Refrigerate dough for half an hour.
★ Drop dough by tablespoons onto an oiled cookie sheet. Press each mound lightly with back of spoon.
★ Bake cookies for 7~10 minutes, until golden.

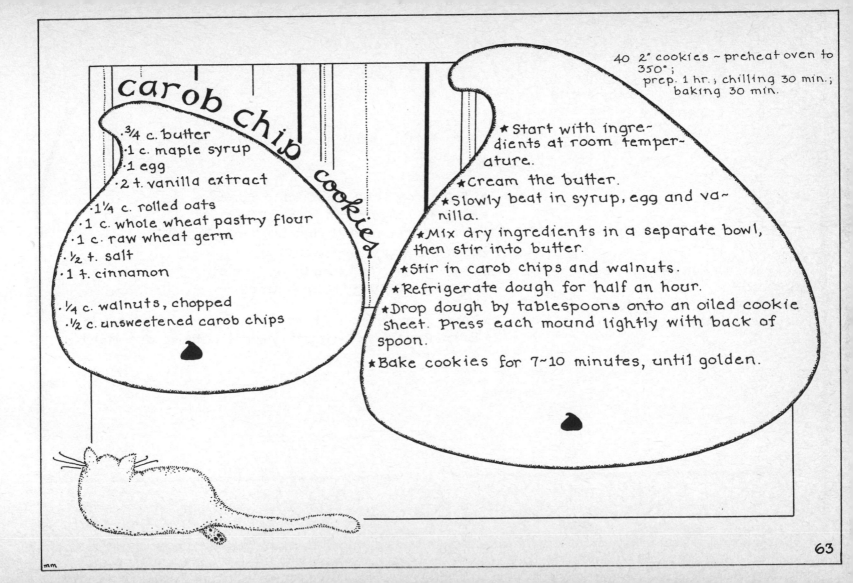

Lemon Pecan
PUFFS

These cookies are deli-
cately flavored and
not very sweet ~ good
for an afternoon tea.

2 doz. cookies ~ preheat oven to 325°;
prep. 45 min.; chilling 30 min.; baking 30 min.

· ½ c. butter
· 2 T. honey
· grated rind of one lemon
· 2 t. lemon juice

· 1 c. whole wheat pastry flour
· pinch salt
· ½ c. pecans, finely chopped
· 24 pecan halves

★ Cream together butter and honey.
★ Beat in lemon rind and juice.
★ Mix flour and salt and beat into butter.
★ Stir in chopped pecans.
★ Chill dough for ½ hour or longer.
★ Set out walnut~sized mounds on an oiled cookie
 sheet.
★ Press one pecan half onto the top of each cookie.
★ Bake for 15~20 minutes, until bottoms are lightly
 browned.

MF

Ginger COOKIES

30 large cookies
preheat oven to 325°;
prep. 45 min.; chilling
30 min.; baking 40 min.

- ¾ c. butter
- 1 c. honey
- 2 eggs
- 2 T. fresh ginger root, chopped
- ½ c. blackstrap molasses

- 3½ c. whole wheat flour
- ½ c. wheat germ
- 1½ t. baking soda
- 1½ t. cinnamon
- 1 t. cloves

★ Cream butter, then beat in honey.

★ Lightly beat eggs and stir into butter.

★ Peel ginger root and chop small enough to measure. Then puree with molasses in blender or food processor, and add to butter mixture.

★ Mix dry ingredients together in a separate bowl.

★ Combine wet and dry ingredients.

★ Chill dough for ½ hour.

★ Drop well-rounded tablespoons of cookie dough onto an oiled cookie sheet. Dipping the spoon in cold water after each cookie is dropped will keep batter from sticking to spoon.

★ Bake cookies for 18~20 minutes on top rack of oven.

Brownies, Bars

AND Other Little Things

Chocolate Walnut brownies

9 2½" brownies ~ preheat oven to 325°
1 oiled 8" x 8" baking pan
prep. 30 min. ; baking 30 ~ 40 min.

· 2½ oz. unsweetened chocolate
· ¼ c. orange juice
· 1½ t. vanilla extract
· 1¼ c. maple syrup
· ½ c. butter
· 2 eggs

· 1 c. whole wheat pastry flour, sifted and then measured
· 1½ t. baking powder
· pinch salt

· ½ c. walnuts, finely chopped

★ Melt chocolate in a double boiler.
★ Cool chocolate briefly, then add orange juice, vanilla and maple syrup.
★ Cream butter and eggs together. Slowly beat in cooled chocolate mixture.
★ Mix dry ingredients together in a large bowl.
★ Pour wet ingredients into dry, mixing thoroughly but briefly.
★ Stir in half of the walnuts.
★ Pour batter into oiled pan.
★ Sprinkle remaining nuts over batter.
★ Bake 30 ~ 40 minutes.
★ Remove from oven when a few crumbs still remain on a knife inserted in the center of pan. Underbaking slightly makes moist, fudgy brownies.

Chocolate Cream Cheese
brownies

12 2"x3" brownies ~ preheat oven to 325°
1 oiled 9"x9" baking pan

prep. 45 min. ; baking 30~40 min.

* Follow recipe for Chocolate Walnut Brownies, page 68.
* Omit **walnuts**.
* Beat **3/4 lb. cream cheese** until soft. Beat in **½ c. maple syrup** and **1 t. vanilla ex~tract**.
* Pour half of the brownie batter into 9"x9" oiled pan.
* Spread cream cheese on top and lightly swirl it into batter with a knife.
* Spread remaining brownie batter on top.
* Bake as directed.

Chocolate Mint
brownies

These brownies make your mouth tingle!

* Follow recipe for Chocolate Walnut Brownies, page 68.
* Reduce **vanilla extract** to ½ t. Add **3/8 t. pure peppermint extract** to batter.
* Walnuts are optional.

Chocolate Frosted
brownies

Frosting brownies turns them into fudgy cake squares.

* Prepare Chocolate Walnut Brownies, page 68. Set aside half of the walnuts.
* Prepare **⅓ recipe of Chocolate Cream Cheese Frosting**, page 149.
* Spread frosting on cooled brownies. Sprinkle walnuts on top. Cut brownies after frosting.

MF

Carob Brownies

9 2½" brownies ~ preheat oven to 325°
1 oiled 8" x 8" baking pan
prep. 30 min. ; baking 30 min.

A distinctively delicious brownie and a great alternative to chocolate.

- ½ c. butter
- ¼ c. honey
- ¼ c. maple syrup
- 2 eggs
- 1 t. vanilla extract

- ½ c. carob powder
- ½ c. whole wheat
  pastry flour
- 1 t. baking powder
- ¼ c. ground almonds
  (optional)

* Start with all ingredients at room temperature.

* Cream butter. Beat in sweeteners, eggs and vanilla.

* Sift carob powder and flour, and mix with baking powder.

* Combine dry and wet ingredients.

* Pour batter into oiled pan.

* Sprinkle nuts on top.

* Bake 25~30 minutes.

* Remove from oven while still a bit soft in the center.

maple Almond BARS

18 1½" x 3" bars
preheat oven to 325°
1 oiled 9" x 9" baking pan
prep. 30 min. ; baking 25~35 min.

- ½ c. butter, softened
- 1 c. maple syrup
- 2 eggs
- ½ t. vanilla extract
- ¼ t. almond extract

- ½ c. ground toasted almonds
- ½ c. whole wheat pastry flour, sifted and then measured
- 2 t. baking powder

★ Cream butter and maple syrup.
★ Beat in eggs and vanilla and almond extracts.
★ Mix dry ingredients in a separate bowl, then combine with wet in~gredients. Mix thoroughly but briefly.
★ Pour batter into prepared pan.
★ Bake for 25~35 minutes until a toothpick in~serted in the center comes out clean.
★ Cut into bars when cooled.

Use a darker grade of maple syrup if available. The flavor will be stronger and richer without being overly~sweet.

CHOCOLATE maple Almond Bars
~ for people who can't resist putting chocolate in everything~

★ Follow recipe for Maple Almond Bars, this page.
★ Add ½ c. **unsweetened cocoa** to dry ingredients.
★ Increase **baking powder** to **1 T.**

Date BARS

18 1½" x 3" bars
preheat oven to 350°
1 oiled 9"x9" baking pan
prep. 50 min. ; baking 30 min.

- 1 c. whole wheat pastry flour
- 2 c. rolled oats
- 1 t. baking powder
- pinch salt
- 1 t. cinnamon
- ½ t. ground ginger
- pinch grated nutmeg
- ½ c. butter, melted
- ⅜ c. maple syrup or honey
- 1 t. vanilla extract
- ¼ t. almond extract
- Date Filling, page 151

★ Mix dry and wet ingredients, each in a separate bowl; then combine and stir well.

★ Press ½ the mixture into the bottom of oiled pan.

★ Prepare Date Filling and spread it on top of the bottom crust.

★ Sprinkle remaining crust over the filling and gently pat it smooth. Make sure the top crust reaches to the edges and corners of pan.

★ Bake for 30 minutes or until golden brown.

★ Cool completely before cutting into bars or they'll crumble.

72

Apricot Bars

18 1½" x 3" bars ~ preheat oven to 350°
1 oiled 9" x 9" baking pan
prep. 50 min.; soaking 1 hr.; baking 30 min.

More exotic than Date Bars; unfortunately also more expensive. Use unsulphured apricots; though a bit drier and less brightly colored than commercial fruit, they are more healthful and work fine in this recipe.

- Crust from Date Bars recipe, page 72

Apricot Filling:

- 1 c. dried apricots
- 1 c. boiling water
- ⅛ ~ ¼ c. maple syrup or honey
- ½ t. vanilla extract (optional)
- ⅛ t. almond extract (optional)
- 1 t. arrowroot mixed with 1 T. water (optional)

★ Lay apricots in a flat dish and pour boiling water over them. Soak fruit for one hour until very soft.
★ Meanwhile, prepare crust, omitting cinnamon, ginger and nutmeg.
★ Drain fruit but save soaking water.
★ Chop soft fruit and purée it in a blender or food processor with sweetener and only as much soaking water as needed for blending.
★ Add extracts if desired.
★ Filling may be thick enough as is. However, if it seems at all runny, bring it to a simmer in a saucepan and stir in arrowroot to thicken.
★ Follow directions in Date Bars recipe for making bars and baking.

73

Chocolate Fudge Nut Bars

18 1½" x 3" bars ~ preheat oven to 350°
1 oiled 9" x 9" baking pan
prep. 1¼ hr.; baking 15 min.

- ½ crust from Date Bar recipe, page 72

- 5 oz unsweetened chocolate
- ¼ c. butter
- 1 c. honey
- ½ c. milk
- 1½ t. vanilla extract
- ¼ t. almond extract
- ½ c. walnuts, chopped

★ Prepare crust as in Date Bars but cut recipe in half. Omit **spices** and use **honey** instead of maple syrup.

★ Press all of the crust into bottom of oiled pan and bake for 10-15 minutes until the edges are lightly browned. Overbaking will cause crumbling, so beware.

★ While crust is baking, melt chocolate and butter in a double boiler.

★ Add honey and heat 5 more minutes.

★ Stir the milk in slowly and continue cooking for 15 minutes until very hot.

★ Then put top of double boiler directly on high heat and quickly bring chocolate to a rolling boil, stirring constantly.

★ As soon as chocolate begins to boil rapidly, lower heat so chocolate stays at a rolling boil but does not burn. Boil for 4~5 minutes, stirring only occasionally.

★ Remove from heat; stir in extracts and half the walnuts.

★ Pour fudge hot over baked crust and spread smooth. Sprinkle remaining nuts on top.

★ Cool completely before cutting into bars.

APPLE fudge BARS

- crust from Date Bar recipe, page 72
- 5 oz unsweetened chocolate
- ¼ c. butter
- 1 c. honey
- ½ c. + 2 T. milk
- 1 t. vanilla extract
- ¼ t. almond extract
- ½ c. dried apple rings
- Apple Glaze, page 154

* Prepare crust, omitting cinnamon and ginger. Press all but ¾ c. crust into baking pan. Spread the extra ¾ c. loosely in second pan. Bake both pans at 350° for 10~12 minutes until golden at edges.
* Melt chocolate and butter in a double boiler.
* Add honey and heat for 5 minutes.
* Add milk and continue heating for 10~15 minutes.
* Then place top of double boiler directly on heat and quickly bring to a rolling boil, stirring often.
* Lower heat so chocolate continues to boil, but doesn't burn. Boil hard for 5 minutes, stirring only occasionally.
* Remove from heat and stir in vanilla and almond extracts.
* Crumble extra crust and mix it into fudge.
* Pour fudge onto the main crust and chill until firm.
* Place apple rings on top of chilled fudge. Lay them flat or make an overlapping pattern.
* Prepare apple glaze and pour it hot over the dried apples.
* Refrigerate several hours until glaze is hard.
* Cut bars small, as they are quite rich.

18 1½" x 3" bars
preheat oven to 350°
2 oiled 9"x9" baking pans
prep. 1½ hr. ; baking 10~12 min. ; chilling 4 hr

raspberry cashew shortbread

9 3" squares ~ preheat oven to 375°
1 oiled 9"x9" baking pan
prep. 45 min.; baking 15 min.

- ½ c. butter
- 3 T. maple syrup

- ¾ c. cashews
- 1 c. whole wheat pastry flour, sifted and then measured
- ¼ t. baking powder
- 2½ oz. raspberry preserves, honey~sweetened if available

★ Start with all ingredients at room tem~perature.

★ Cream butter until smooth.

★ Beat in maple syrup.

★ Using a blender or food processor, grind ½ cup of the cashews into a powder. Mix with the flour and baking powder.

★ Beat dry ingredients into the butter.

★ Spread batter into oiled pan and bake for 15 minutes.

★ Spread preserves on cooled short~bread.

★ Finely chop remaining cashews and sprinkle them on top.

★ Cut into squares.

jam

mm

Shortbread

1 lb. of shortbread ~ preheat oven to 350°;
1 buttered 9"x 9" baking pan; prep. 25 min.;
baking 25 min.

- 2/3 c. butter
- 1/3 c. maple syrup **OR** maple syrup and honey combined
- 2 1/3 c. whole wheat pastry flour

* Start with ingredients at room temperature.

* Cream butter with sweeteners until smooth.

* Sift flour before measuring, then beat it into butter.

* Spread batter into buttered pan.

* Bake for 25 minutes until edges begin to brown.

* Cut into squares or triangles.

Chocolate Covered Shortbread

18 1 1/2" x 3" bars ; prep. 1 hr.

Prepare Shortbread, this page, as directed. While it bakes, prepare Chocolate Topping:

- 2 oz. unsweetened chocolate
- 1 T. butter
- 1 c. honey
- 1/4 t. vanilla extract
- 1/2 c. walnuts, coarsely chopped

* Melt chocolate and butter in a double boiler.

* Add honey and heat 5 more minutes.

* Put top of double boiler directly on heat, and cook chocolate at a rolling boil for 3 minutes on medium heat.

* Remove from heat, stir in vanilla, and pour over baked shortbread.

* Sprinkle with walnuts and chill.

* Cut into bars.

fig FREWTON bars

18 1½" x 3" bars
preheat oven to 350°
2 oiled 9" x 9" bak~
ing pans
prep.1 hr.; baking 15 min.

Cookie:
- 1 c. butter
- ½ c. maple syrup
- 2 eggs
- 1 t. vanilla extract
- 2½ c. whole wheat pastry flour, sifted and then measured
- ¼ t. salt

Filling:
- 1 c. dried figs
- 3 T. maple syrup
- 2 t. lemon juice
- 2 t. butter, melted
- ¾ c. water

★Start with all ingre~ dients at room tempera~ ture.

★Cream butter. Slowly beat in maple, eggs and vanilla.

★Mix flour and salt, and beat into batter.

★Spread batter into 2 oiled pans, and bake for 10~15 minutes until cookie begins to separate from the edges of pan.

★Purée figs in a blender or food processor with all other filling ingredients.

★Gently simmer figs for 5~10 minutes.

★Take one pan and turn cookie upside down onto a platter.

★Spread all the filling onto it.

★Lay second cookie, right side up, on top of the filling.

★Carefully cut into bars.

78

Walnut Gingerbread

· 1 c. butter
· ½ c. honey
· ⅔ c. blackstrap molasses
· ¾ c. maple syrup
· 2 t. vanilla extract
· 3 eggs

· 5 c. whole wheat pastry flour
· 1 T. baking soda
· 1 t. salt
· 2½ T. powdered ginger
· 2 t. cinnamon
· 2 t. ground nutmeg
· ½ t. dry mustard
· 2 c. milk
· 1½ c. walnuts, chopped

15 2½" x 3" pieces ~ preheat oven to 350°
1 oiled 9" x 13" baking pan
prep. 30 min. ; baking 45 min.

★Start with all ingredients at room temperature.

★Cream butter, then beat in sweeteners until smooth.

★Beat in vanilla and eggs.

★Mix dry ingredients together and combine with butter mixture in 3 segments, alternating with the milk. Beat until smooth.

★Stir in walnuts.

★Pour batter into oiled pan and bake for 45 minutes, until a toothpick inserted in center of pan just comes out dry. Take care not to overbake so the gingerbread will not dry out too quickly.

79

peanut butter
fudge

16 2" pieces
1 buttered 8"x 8" baking pan
prep. 30 min.

- 1½ c. maple syrup
- ¾ c. milk
- 4 T. crunchy natural peanut butter
- 1 t. vanilla extract
- pinch salt
- ⅓ c. chopped peanuts (optional)

★ Mix syrup and milk together in a large saucepan.

★ Boil mixture on high heat without stirring until it reaches 238° on a candy thermo~meter (soft ball stage). This will take 10~15 minutes.

★ Remove from heat and cool.

★ Mix peanut butter, vanilla, salt and peanuts together.

★ Beat peanut butter into cooled syrup with a wooden spoon. Beat until it loses its gloss.

★ Pat fudge into buttered pan and smooth with the spoon or your hand.

★ Mark it into squares and let it cool several hours before cutting.

Popcorn Balls

- 1 c. unpopped corn or 28 c. popped popcorn
- 1 c. barley malt syrup (see Sweeteners, page 13)
- 2 T. blackstrap molasses (optional)
- 3 T. butter

★ Pop corn. Separate out and discard any un-popped kernels.

★ Bring barley malt, molasses and 2 T. of the butter to a rolling boil. Cook for 3 minutes or until mixture reaches 220° on a candy thermometer.

★ Remove from heat, pour over popcorn, and stir with a spoon.

★ As soon as corn is cool enough to handle, grease your hands with remaining butter and press mixture into balls. Do this quickly or barley malt will become too brittle to shape. Young children have fun helping out here ~ just grease their hands well.

81

Candied Brandied Pecans

- 1 c. pecans, shelled whole pieces
- ¼ c. brandy
- ¼ c. maple syrup
- 2 T. butter
- ⅛ t. salt (optional)

★ Soak pecans in brandy for 10 minutes.

★ Stir in maple syrup.

★ Melt butter and pour in pecan

★ Simmer for 5~10 minutes, stirring constantly, until most of the liquid has boiled away and what remains is golden brown and very thick.

★ Spread pecans onto a piece of wax paper to cool.

★ Sprinkle with salt while they are still warm.

★ Use them to decorate a cake or serve as a snack food.

PASTRIES

Éclairs

Making éclair shells is surprisingly easy, so don't be intimidated by the idea ~ all you need is a pastry bag. But don't attempt this recipe in very humid weather be~ cause the shells won't puff.

· ½ recipe Egg Custard Filling, page 151
· 5 eggs, at room temperature
· 1 c. sifted whole wheat pastry flour
· ⅓ c. butter
· 1 c. milk
· 1~2 T. maple syrup or honey
· Semi~Sweet Chocolate Glaze, page 154

★ Prepare Egg Custard Filling. Set it aside to cool.

★ Beat eggs and set them aside in a warm place.

★ Sift flour several times to sift out the coarser flecks of bran. Measure flour after sifting.

★ Melt butter in a heavy~bottomed sauce~ pan. Add milk and sweetener.

★ When mixture begins to boil add the flour all at once, and beat with a wooden spoon until the dough is smooth and no longer clings to the sides of the pan or the spoon. This will only take about 30 seconds; then remove from heat.

*Beat in beaten eggs, about one egg at a time, making sure that each one is well incorporated into the dough before adding the next.

*Spoon dough into a pastry bag. Using a tip with a fairly large opening, squeeze dough onto an oiled baking sheet in 3″ x 1½″ strips. End each strip with an upward, slightly backward motion of the pastry bag. This makes a rounded end without a tail.

*Bake at 400° for 10 minutes, then reduce oven temperature to 350° and bake an additional 20~25 minutes. Don't open the oven door while shells are baking or the pastry will lose its puff. Shells are done when they hold their shape completely when pressed.

*Cool éclairs, then cut them almost all the way through horizontally with a serrated knife.

*Prepare Semi~Sweet Chocolate Glaze. Cool glaze until it begins to thicken, then pour or brush over pastry shells.

*Spoon 3 tablespoons of filling into each éclair just before serving.

Chocolate Poppy Seed Roll

~ where chocolate lovers and poppy seed lovers meet ~

12 pastries ~ preheat oven to 425°
1 oiled cookie sheet
prep 1¼ hr.; baking 30 min.

· 1 Whole Wheat Pastry Crust, page 116
· ¾ c. + 1t. poppy seeds
· ¼ c. milk
· ½ c. honey
· ½ c. cream cheese
· 1 oz. unsweetened chocolate

Egg Wash:

· 1 egg white
· 1 T. water
· 1 t. honey

* Prepare pastry dough, adding 1~2 T. extra maple syrup if desired. Refrigerate.
* Grind ¾ c. of poppy seeds using a hand or electric grinder or a blender.
* Combine seeds, milk and honey in a saucepan and simmer over moder~ ate heat for 4 minutes. Stir constantly to avoid burning.
* Remove from heat and beat in cream cheese with a wooden spoon.
* Melt chocolate in a double boiler and stir into poppy seed mixture.
* Roll out pie dough on a well~floured surface to a 10" x 15" rectangle.
* Spread filling over dough, leaving a ½" margin on one long side.
* Roll dough up, starting along the other long side.
* Brush the end margin with water and press it to the roll to close it.
* With spatulas underneath for support, transfer the roll onto cookie sheet.
* With a fork, lightly beat together egg wash ingredients.
* Brush egg wash over roll and sprinkle with remaining poppy seeds.
* Bake in a preheated 425° oven for 10 minutes. Then reduce heat to 350° and continue baking 20 minutes longer.
* When roll is completely cool, cut in ¾" slices with a finely~serrated knife, or bring it whole to the table.

Hamentashen

These lovely 3-sided pastries are traditionally baked for the Jewish holiday of Purim, and are filled with a poppy seed or fruit filling.

40 pastries ~ preheat oven to 350°
1 oiled cookie sheet
prep. 1½ hr. ; chilling 1 hr. ; baking 30 min.

Poppy Seed Filling, page 153, or
Apricot Filling, page 73, or
Marzipan Filling, page 152, or
any fruit preserves
- ½ c. butter
- ⅜ maple syrup
- 2 eggs
- 2½ c. whole wheat pastry flour
- 1½ t. baking powder

Egg wash:
- 1 egg white, lightly beaten
- 1 T. water
- 1 t. honey or maple syrup

★ Prepare filling and set aside to cool.

★ Cream butter until smooth.

★ Beat in maple syrup and eggs.

★ Mix flour and baking powder together and add to the wet ingredients. Mix thoroughly.

★ Chill dough at least 1 hour.

★ Roll dough out on a floured board to ⅛" thickness.

★ Cut into 2½" rounds with a flour-dipped cutter.

★ Place 1½ t. of filling in the center of each round and draw up three sides together, pinching edges closed.

★ Set on an oiled cookie sheet.

★ Brush tops with egg wash.

★ Bake for 30 minutes.

Danish Pastry

20 pastries ~ preheat oven to 375°
1 oiled cookie sheet
prep. 2¼ hr. ; chilling 5¼ hr. or
1¼ hr. + overnight ; baking
25 min.

- 2 T. baking yeast
- ¼ c. water
- ½ c. honey
- ½ c. milk
- 2 eggs, lightly beaten
- 1 lb. butter, unsalted
- 1 t. vanilla extract
- 5½ c. sifted whole wheat pastry flour
- 1 t. salt
- ½ t. freshly-ground cardamon, or 1 t. preground
- 1 egg white

Cheese Filling:
- 1 c. cream cheese
- ½ c. maple syrup
- 2 c. ricotta cheese
- ½ t. grated lemon rind
- 1 t. lemon juice
- 1 t. vanilla

or :
- Poppy Seed Filling, page 153

or :
- 12 oz. jam, honey~sweetened if available

Making Danish pastry is a rather involved project, but taken step by step it is fairly easy. The dough is amazingly elastic and easy to handle for whole wheat. This recipe is purposely large, as the unbaked pastry can be frozen and baked fresh when desired.

★Dissolve yeast in warm water. Stir in ¼ c. of honey.

★ Set in a warm place for 10 minutes, until yeast begins to bubble.

★ In a second bowl combine remaining honey, milk, eggs, 1 T. of melted but~ter, and vanilla extract.

★ Sift flour, separating out and discard~ing largest flecks of bran. Measure after sifting.

★ Mix 4¼ c. flour with salt and carda~mon.

90

★ Stir liquid mixture into yeast. Add dry mix.

★ Knead dough for 5 minutes on a floured surface, incorporating ½ to ¾ c. more sifted flour into dough. Dough should be light and moist.

★ Lightly dust kneaded ball of dough with flour, wrap in aluminum foil and refrigerate for 45 minutes.

★ Warm butter and whip until it is light and soft.

Roll dough out on floured surface to a large rectangle measuring about 12"x 17."

★ Spread ¼ lb. butter over ⅔ of the rectangle (1). Fold the unbuttered third over the center third of the rectangle (2), then fold again over the rest (3).

★ Lightly re-flour the surface, rotate the dough ¼ turn (4), and roll it out again to same size. Repeat buttering, folding and rotating process 3 more times until all the butter is used.

★ Wrap folded dough in aluminum foil and refrigerate for 4 hours or overnight.

★ Prepare filling. For Cheese Filling, blend cream cheese and syrup with a wooden spoon. Stir in ricotta cheese, grated lemon rind, lemon juice and vanilla. Refrigerate until needed.

Continued on next page.

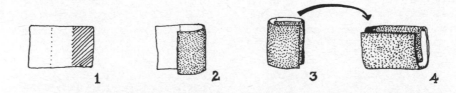

1   2   3   4

★ Cut dough in half. Roll out one half of the dough to an ⅛"~¼" thick 12"x 17" rectangle.

★ Spread half the filling over the dough, leaving a 1" edge uncovered along the long side. Roll up dough, ending with that edge. Brush edge with water and press onto roll.

★ Using spatulas for support, move roll onto a flour~dusted cookie sheet. Refrigerate for at least 30 minutes.

★ Repeat process with remaining half of the dough.

★ Cut chilled roll into 1"~wide slices. Lay them on an oiled cookie sheet, leaving only about 1" of space between them.

★ Bake for 15 minutes. Remove from oven, brush pastries with a lightly~beaten egg white and return to oven for 7 more minutes, or until lightly browned.

★ For jam~filled pastries, spread 4~5 oz. of jam over each rolled half of dough. Roll along short edge to make a thicker, shorter roll. At the same time that the egg white is brushed over pastries, place a dab of jam in each center.

Bake only as many pastries as will be eaten immediately. Dough can be refrigerated for several days or frozen indefinitely. Freeze rolls in sections, only as large as will be used at one time, so they can be thawed and baked in small batches. Thaw overnight. Slice and bring pastry to room temperature before baking.

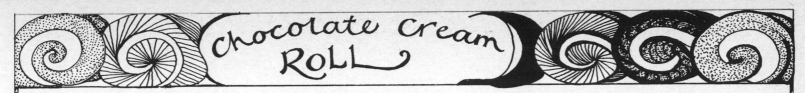

Chocolate Cream ROLL

~ simple yet elegant ~

8 servings ~ preheat oven to 375°
1 oiled 10½" x 15½" pan;
prep. 1 hr.; baking 12 min.; chilling 1 hr.

· ¼ c. unsweetened cocoa
· ¾ c. whole wheat pastry flour, sifted and then measured
· 1 t. baking powder

· 4 eggs, separated
· ¼ c. + 2 T. honey
· 1 t. vanilla extract
· 1 T. rum (optional)
· 1¼ c. heavy cream
· 2 T. maple syrup
· ½ t. vanilla extract or Kirsch

* Mix cocoa, sifted flour and baking powder.
* Beat egg yolks until they are very thick and creamy~ about 10 or 15 minutes. Add honey, 1 t. vanilla and rum slowly while beating.
* Gradually add dry ingredients and beat until smooth.
* Beat egg whites until stiff but not dry, and fold them into batter.
* Spread batter into oiled pan. It will be very thin.
* Bake for 10~12 minutes.
* Cool cake for a few minutes, then loosen the edges with a knife. Place a towel over the cake and with two spatulas placed under one end of the cake roll it up into the towel.
* Chill cake rolled up in towel in refrigerator for 1 hour.
* Whip cream until stiff, then beat in maple syrup and vanilla or Kirsch.
* Unroll the cake, remove the towel, and spread whipped cream over cake.
* Re~roll cake, placing seam side down.
* Chill for at least 15 minutes before slicing.

Pies

peach custard pie

* Prepare pie dough. Roll out bottom crust and place in pie plate. Refrigerate crust and remaining dough.

* Skin peaches by dropping them a few at a time into boiling water. Cook for 2 minutes and then plunge them into a bowl of ice water. The loosened skins will pull right off.

* Slice peaches and drain the slices in a colander for 10 minutes. Catch the juice for a refreshing drink!

* In a blender or food processor whip honey, the three whole eggs, nutmeg and arrowroot until smooth.

* Combine well-drained peaches and blended mixture and pour into bottom crust.

* Roll out remaining dough. Cover pie with top crust. Flute the edges and brush with lightly-beaten egg white. Prick holes in the top crust with a fork. Bake at 425° for 10 minutes. Reduce heat to 350° and bake an additional 30 minutes.

* Cool pie for at least one hour before cutting.

· 2 Whole Wheat Pastry Crusts, page 116
· 3½ ~ 4 lbs peaches
· ½ ~ ¾ c. honey
· 3 eggs
· 1 egg white
· ¼ t. grated nutmeg
· 4 T. arrowroot

96

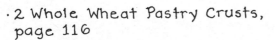

Apple pie

8~10 servings ~ preheat oven to 450°; 1 10" pie plate; prep. 2 hr.; baking 45 min.

- 2 Whole Wheat Pastry Crusts, page 116
- 10 c. peeled, cored and sliced baking apples
- ⅓ c. honey
- 2 T. arrowroot
- 1 T. lemon juice
- 1¼ t. cinnamon
- ¼ t. grated nutmeg
- 1 egg white

★ Prepare pie dough. Roll out bottom crust and line pie plate with it. Refrigerate rolled crust and remaining dough.

★ Fill bottom crust with apples. They will be heaped up very high.

★ Mix honey, arrowroot, lemon juice and spices together until completely blended and pour evenly over apples.

★ Roll out remaining dough for top crust.

★ Cover pie with top crust and flute the edges. Brush crust with lightly~beaten egg white and prick fork holes in it so steam can escape.

★ Bake at 450° for 10 minutes, then reduce temperature to 350° and bake an additional 25~35 minutes. Apples should feel soft, but not mushy, to an inserted knife. Cool before cutting.

97

Apple Raisin PIE

8~10 servings
preheat oven to 425°
1 10" pie plate
prep 1¾ hr.; cooling 30 min.;
baking 35 min.

- 2½ c. raisins
- 1 c. apple cider or juice
- 1 c. water
- 2 unbaked Whole Wheat Pastry Crusts, page 116
- 3 eggs, well beaten
- 2 T. molasses
- 1 t. lemon extract
- 2 t. powdered ginger
- ¼ t. ground cloves
- juice of 1 lemon (about ¼ c.)
- 1 T. whole wheat pastry flour
- 2 or 3 large baking apples

★ Place raisins in top of a double boiler. Add cider and water and soak for 30 minutes.

★ Prepare pie dough. Roll out one crust and line pie plate with it. Refrigerate crust and remaining dough.

★ Add to raisins all ingredients except flour and apples.

★ Heat in double boiler, stirring frequently.

★ Sift flour twice, separating out and discarding the coarsest bran each time. Measure flour after sifting.

★ As filling begins to thicken, sprinkle in flour and stir until thick.

★ Remove filling from heat and cool completely.

★ Peel, core and slice apples.

★ Line the bottom crust with apple slices, then cover with raisin filling.

★ Cover pie with a lattice crust (see pages 118~19).

★ Bake at 425° for 10 minutes. Reduce heat to 350° and bake an additional 25 minutes. Cool before cutting.

Apple Rhubarb pie

8~10 servings ~ preheat oven to 400°
1 10" pie plate
prep 2 hr. ; baking 40 min.

This pie has the tart early summer spirit of the rhubarb.

· 2 Whole Wheat Pastry Crusts, page 116
· 5 cups cut rhubarb (1" pieces)
· 4½ c. peeled, cored and sliced baking apples
· ¾ ~ 1 c. honey
· 3 eggs, well~beaten
· 3 T. arrowroot
· 1 egg white

★ Prepare pie dough. Roll out one crust and line pie plate. Refrigerate crust and remaining dough.

★ Cut fruits; mix apples and rhubarb together, and place in pie plate.

★ Mix honey, eggs and arrowroot together, making sure to break up any lumps of arrowroot, and pour it over fruit.

★ Roll out remaining dough and weave a lattice crust (see pages 118~19) across the top of the pie. Flute the edges.

★ Lightly beat the egg white and brush onto lattice crust.

★ Bake at 400° for 10 minutes; then reduce heat to 350° and continue baking for another 25~30 minutes.

Try substituting sliced strawberries for all or part of the apples.

Concord Grape Pie

An Autumn harvest treat.
Concord grape season is short;
extra fruit can be prepared and
frozen for another time of year.

8~10 servings ~ preheat oven to 425°
1 10" pie plate
prep 1¾ hr.; baking 1 hr.; cooling
2 hr.

· 2 Whole Wheat Pie
Crusts, page 116
· 7 c. ripe Concord grapes
· ⅔ c. maple syrup
· 4 T. arrowroot

★ Prepare pie dough. Roll out 1 crust and place in pie plate.
Refrigerate crust and remaining dough.
★ Wash and drain grapes.
★ Separate skins from pulp by lightly squeezing each grape. The pulp
will pop right out. Save pulp and skins.
★ Cook pulps over high heat for 5 minutes, stirring constantly.
★ Sieve pulps through a food mill to separate out the seeds. Discard seeds.
★ Combine seedless pulp and grape skins.
★ Mix maple syrup with arrowroot until smooth. Add to fruit.
★ Pour mixture into bottom crust.
★ Roll out top crust and weave a lattice (see pages 118~19) across the top.
Flute the edges and brush with an egg white wash.
★ Bake at 425° for 10 minutes. Then reduce oven temperature to 350°
and bake an additional 50 minutes.
★ Cool pie completely before cutting.

Cherry pie

8~10 servings ~ preheat oven to 425°; 1 10" pie plate.
prep. 1¾ hr.; baking 50 min.

· 2 Whole Wheat Pastry
Crusts, page 116
· 6 c. pitted sweet cherries
(a bit less than 3 lbs. of
whole fresh cherries)
· ¾ c. honey
· 3 T. arrowroot
· 2 T. cherry juice, apple juice,
or any non~citrus fruit juice
· 1 T. cherry brandy or cherry
liqueur.
· 2 t. lemon juice
· 1 egg white

★ Prepare pastry dough. Roll out one crust and place in
pie plate. Refrigerate crust and remaining dough.
★ Wash, pit and halve cherries. Drain off any juice.
★ Add honey to cherries.
★ Mix together arrowroot, juice, brandy and lemon juice,
then add to cherries.
★ Pour fruit into bottom crust.
★ Roll out remaining pie dough and weave a lattice
crust (see pages 118~19).
★ Lightly beat egg white and brush onto lattice crust
with a pastry brush.
★ Bake at 425° for 10 minutes. Reduce temperature
to 350° and bake an additional 40 minutes, until
set.
★ Cool before cutting.

Blueberry pie

★ Follow recipe for Cherry Pie, this page.
★ Substitute **6 c. fresh blueberries** for cherries.
★ Substitute **¼ c. maple syrup** for ¼ c. of the honey.
★ Increase **arrowroot** to **3½ T.**
★ Substitute **orange juice** for cherry juice.

MF

Pumpkin pie

8-10 servings ~ preheat oven to 350°
1 10" pie plate
prep 1 hr.; baking 2 hr.

· 1 unbaked whole wheat pastry crust, page 116.
· 1 small pumpkin (1½ ~ 2 lbs.)
· 4 eggs
· 1 c. maple syrup
· 2 T. blackstrap molasses
· 1 c. heavy cream
· 2 t. vanilla extract
· ¼ t. salt
· 2 t. cinnamon
· 1 t. powdered ginger
· ½ t. ground cloves
· ½ t. allspice
· ¼ t. grated nutmeg
· whipped cream

★ Prepare pie dough. Roll out crust, place in pie plate, flute edges and refrigerate.

★ Cut pumpkin in half horizontally, scoop out the seeds, and place the two halves face down on a baking pan. Put ¼" of water in the bottom of the pan and bake at 350° for one hour, or until soft. Spoon pumpkin pulp out of its skin. Measure out 3 c. of pulp, and freeze the rest for your next pie or for Pumpkin Cheesecake, page 48.

★ Increase oven temperature to 450°.

★ Purée measured pulp with all other ingre~ dients* in a blender or food processor.

★ Pour the mixture into unbaked crust. Bake at 450° for 10 minutes, then reduce oven tem~ perature to 350° and bake an additional 45 minutes, until set.

★ Cool pie before cutting. Serve with whipped cream.

*but not whipped cream!

Make these two pies late into the winter, long after fresh pumpkins are gone from the farm stands. They have the same delightful harvest flavor of pumpkin pie.

Squash Pie

*Follow recipe for Pumpkin Pie, page 102.

*Substitute **3 c. mashed butternut squash** for pumpkin pulp. Bake squash the same as pumpkin, until soft. Extra cooked squash can also be frozen for another pie.

Sweet Potato Pie

*Follow recipe for Pumpkin Pie, page 102.

*Bake or boil about **2½~3 lbs.** of **sweet potatoes** until soft. Skin them and measure out 3½ c. mashed potato.

*Reduce **maple syrup** to ½ c.

Brazilian Fig Pie

10 servings ~ preheat oven to 450°
1 10" pie plate
   prep. 1 hr. ; baking 35 min. ; cooling
    45 min.

- 1 Whole Wheat Pastry Crust, page 116
- ½ c. butter
- 2 c. Brazil nuts, unsalted or rinsed
- 1 c. figs
- ½ c. milk

- 3 eggs
- ¾ c. honey
- 1 T. arrowroot
- 1 t. vanilla extract
- ½ t. ground cardamon

★Prepare crust and pre-bake it (using pie beans, page 117) for 5 minutes at 450°. Remove; reduce heat to 350°.

★Melt butter and set it aside to cool.

★Finely grind Brazil nuts, coarsely chop figs, and mix together.

★Whip all other ingredients, including cooled butter, in a blender or food processor until mixture is light and smooth. Stir blended mix into nuts and figs.

★Pour batter into pre-baked crust and bake at 350° for 35 minutes.

★Cool before cutting.

Maple Walnut PIE

10 servings
preheat oven to 450°
1 9" or 10" pie plate
prep. 50 min.; baking 30 min.

~ a very rich and wonderful pie ~

· 1 Whole Wheat Pastry Crust, page 116
· 2½ c. walnuts
· 1 c. maple syrup (the darker the grade, the better for this pie)
· ½ c. butter, melted and cooled
· 3 eggs, lightly beaten
· 1 t. vanilla extract
· ¼ t. salt
· 2 t. arrowroot

*Prepare crust. Bake it using pie beans, page 117, for 7 minutes at 450°. Remove; lower temperature to 350°.

*Grind walnuts until fairly fine, then combine all ingredients.

*Pour filling into pre-baked crust.

*Bake for 25~30 minutes at 350° until almost firm.

*Cool pie before cutting.

Sunflower Walnut PIE

~ a more healthful, less rich pie than Maple Walnut Pie ~

*Follow recipe for Maple Walnut Pie, this page.
*Substitute 1½ c. ground sunflower seeds for 1½ c. of the walnuts. Use raw, unsalted seeds.
*Substitute ½ c. honey for ½ c. of the maple syrup.

105

butterscotch crunch pie

10 servings ~ preheat oven to
350° ; 1 10" pie plate
prep 1¼ hr. ; chilling 3 hr.

- 1 Granola Crumb Crust, page 121
- 2½ c. milk
- ¾ maple syrup
- 4 t. blackstrap molasses
- 3 T. sifted whole wheat pastry flour (with larger flakes of bran separated out and discarded)
- ¼ c. butter
- ⅜ t. salt
- 3 T. arrowroot mixed with 3 T. water
- 6 egg yolks, beaten
- ¾ t. vanilla extract
- 1 c. granola

★ Prepare crust and pre-bake at 350° for 15 minutes.

★ Scald milk in a saucepan.

★ Heat syrup, molasses, sifted flour, butter and salt in a double boiler.

★ Pour all but ½ c. of the scalded milk into double boiler and whisk briskly.

★ Whisk remaining milk into beaten egg yolk, then whisk into double boiler. Whisk constantly, as custard will begin to thicken immediately.

★ Add arrowroot.

★ Continue cooking in the double boiler and whisking a few minutes longer, until custard is very thick. Then remove from heat and whisk in vanilla.

★ Pour mixture into baked crust.

★ Sprinkle top with granola. If granola isn't very crunchy, you may want to freshen it up a bit by toasting it in a 350° oven for 10 minutes before sprinkling on pie.

★ Refrigerate several hours before cutting.

chocolate Fudge PIE

- 1 Graham Cracker Pie Crust, page 120 or Brownie Almond Crust, page 122.
- 2 T. agar~agar flakes (see Glossary of Ingredients, page 7)
- ¾ c. water
- 3 oz unsweetened chocolate
- 1 c. honey
- 1½ t. vanilla extract
- ¾ t. almond extract
- 3 T. arrowroot
- ¾ c. butter, room temperature
- 4 eggs, separated
- pinch salt
- ¾ c. almonds, sliced or chopped

★ Prepare crust. Do not pre~bake.

★ Boil agar~agar in water until it is completely dissolved.

★ Add chocolate and place saucepan in a double boiler until chocolate is melted.

★ Cool completely. Mixture will become rather rubbery.

★ Whip it in a blender or food processor with the honey, extracts and arrowroot until smooth.

★ Cream the butter with an electric mixer.

★ Beat egg yolks into butter.

★ Slowly beat in chocolate mixture.

★ Whip the egg whites to soft peaks. Whip in salt. Fold whites into filling.

★ Pour into crumb crust and sprinkle almonds on top.

★ Bake at 325° for 30~35 minutes until set.

★ Cool completely before cutting.

107

MF

coconut cream PIE

10 servings ~ preheat oven to 350°
1 10" pie plate ; prep. 50 min. ;
baking 40 min.

- 1 Graham Cracker Pie Crust, page 120
- 2½ c. milk
- ½ c. heavy cream
- 4 T. arrowroot
- ½ c. maple syrup
- 4 eggs
- 1 t. vanilla extract
- ½ c. unsweetened shredded coconut

* Prepare crumb crust and pre~bake for 5 minutes at 425°.

* Heat 2¼ c. milk and all of the cream in a sauce~pan over medium heat.

* Mix remaining ¼ c. milk with arrowroot.

* Whip maple syrup, eggs and vanilla in a blender or food processor.

* When bubbles start to form around the edges of the milk, whisk in arrowroot and whisk constant~ly until the milk thickens; then remove from heat.

* Whisk in the egg mixture.

* Pour filling into pre-baked crust and cover with coconut.

* Bake 30~40 minutes at 350° until custard sets.

These recipes are simple variations on Coconut Cream Pie.

Follow the recipe on the preceding page with these changes:

Chocolate Coconut Cream Pie

* Reduce **milk** to 2¼ c.
* Increase **sweetener** to ¾ c., adding either maple syrup or honey.
* Melt **2½ oz. unsweetened chocolate** in a double boiler. Whisk it into hot milk just before whisking in arrowroot.

Banana Cream Pie

* Reduce **milk** to 2 c.
* Reduce **sweetener** to ⅓ c.
* Blend **2 bananas and a pinch of salt** with the eggs and maple syrup.
* Lay slices of **1 banana** on crust before pouring in custard.
* Omit **coconut**.
* Dust top of pie with freshly-grated **nutmeg**.

Chocolate Banana Cream Pie

* Follow recipe for Banana Cream Pie, this page.
* Melt **2 oz. unsweetened chocolate** in a double boiler and whisk it into hot milk just before whisking in arrowroot.
* Adjust sweetener to taste.

MF

Mint cream pie

These recipes are variations on Coconut Cream Pie, page 108. Follow that recipe with these changes.

★ Add ½ t. pure peppermint extract with vanilla.

★ Omit coconut.

Chocolate Almond cream pie

CHOCOLATE MINT cream pie

Follow recipe for Mint Cream Pie, this page.

Use Brownie Almond Crust, page 122, or Graham Cracker Pie Crust, page 120.

Grate ½ oz unsweetened chocolate over top of baked pie while it is still hot. The chocolate will melt across the top, forming a very thin bittersweet glaze.

Follow Chocolate Coconut Cream Pie variation, page 109.

Use 2 oz. chocolate.

Use 1 t. almond extract, ½ t. vanilla extract and (optional) 1 T. Amaretto.

Replace coconut with ½ c. almond slivers.

110

MF

frozen chocolate custard PIE

10 servings; 1 10" pie plate
prep 1¼ hr.; freezing
1~2 hr.

· 1 Coconut Chocolate Crust,
page 122.
· ⅔ c. maple syrup
· 3 eggs, separated
· ⅓ c. milk
· 1 oz. unsweetened
chocolate, grated
· 1½ c. heavy cream

★ Prepare Coconut Chocolate Crust; bake as directed.

★ In a saucepan cook ⅓ c. of the maple syrup, lightly
beaten egg yolks, milk and grated chocolate over
medium heat.

★ Stir constantly until thickened, then remove from
heat and cool.

★ When custard is completely cool, beat egg whites until
stiff but not dry. Then beat in 3 T. of maple syrup.

★ Whip 1 c. of the cream with remaining 3 T. maple
syrup. Don't bother washing beaters or bowl, as
there is more cream to whip.

★ Transfer the cooled custard to a bowl and fold in
egg whites and whipped cream with a rubber spat~
ula.

★ Pour the filling into well~cooled crust and spread
it smooth.

★ For a final flourish, whip remaining cream until stiff and, using a pastry bag, deco~
rate outside edge of pie (optional). See Decorating Hints, page 22.

★ Freeze pie. Remove from freezer half an hour before serving time.

ice cream pie

Delight your friends on a hot day with this easy and elegant pie.

- 1 Graham Cracker Pie Crust, page 120
- 5½ c. ice cream, any flavor (honey-sweetened if available)

Chocolate Topping:
- 1 oz. unsweetened chocolate
- 3 T. butter
- ⅓ c. maple syrup and honey
- ½ c. walnuts
- ¼ c. heavy cream (optional)

10 servings ~ preheat oven to 350°; 1 10" pie plate; prep. 1½ hr.; freezing 2 hr.

★ Prepare crust. Oil pie plate before pressing crust into it. Bake it at 350° for 10 minutes. Chill completely.

★ Fill pie crust with ice cream, working as quickly as you can. Pack it down with a spoon and smooth the top with a rubber spatula.

★ Freeze pie for at least one hour.

★ Meanwhile, make the topping by melting chocolate and butter in a double boiler and then adding sweetener.

★ Chop walnuts rather fine.

★ Pour partially-cooled sauce over frozen pie, sprinkle walnuts over top and quickly return to freezer.

★ Let chocolate sauce harden.

★ Then, whip cream until stiff. Using a pastry bag, decorate outside edge of the pie (optional). See page 22 for decorating hints. Return pie to freezer.

★ Ice cream pie can be frozen almost indefinitely. Wrap in a plastic bag after whipped cream is frozen solid.

★ice cream pie Toppings ★ ★ ★ ★

Prepare Ice Cream Pie, page 112, without Chocolate Topping. Freeze for 1 hour.

Banana~Coconut topping

- 2 large bananas
- 1 c. heavy cream
- 2 T. maple syrup
- rum to taste
- ½ c. shredded unsweetened coconut

★ Cover ice cream~filled pie with sliced bananas.

★ Whip cream until stiff, then whip in maple syrup and rum (optional).

★ Spread ¾ of whipped cream over bananas. Return pie to freezer.

★ Toast coconut until it starts to brown. Cool, then sprinkle onto whipped cream.

★ Using a pastry bag, decorate outside edge of pie with remaining whipped cream (optional ~ see page 22 for decorating hints).

★ Freeze before serving.

Almond~Fruit topping

- ½ c. fruit glaze, pages 154~55, or fruit syrup, pages 160~61
- ¼ ~ ½ c. toasted almond slivers
- ¼ c. heavy cream (optional)

★ Prepare glaze or syrup, cool partially, and spread on ice cream ~ filled pie.

★ Cover with almonds.

★ Whip cream until stiff. Using a pastry bag, decorate outside edge of pie (optional ~ see page 22).

Fresh Fruit topping

★ Cover ice cream filled pie with fresh fruit. Refreeze or serve.

★ Decorate with whipped cream. Refreeze or serve.

Whole Wheat Pastry Pie Crust

1 10" pie plate
prep. 30 min.

~Yes, it is possible to make a light, flaky pie crust with whole wheat flour. It requires quick yet careful handling, well~chilled ingredients, and the right type of whole wheat flour. See Baking Hints, pages 15~17.

· 1 c. whole wheat pastry flour
· ⅓ c. butter
· 1 T. maple syrup
· ¼ c. ice water

* Chill all ingredients before starting. For an extra~flaky crust, use frozen butter.
* Cut butter into flour, using 2 knives, a pastry cutter or a grater, until pieces of butter are pea~sized.
* Mix in maple syrup, working it very lightly with your fingers.
* Add ice water, 1 T. at a time, and toss the dough light~ly through your fingers to mix. Avoid pressing the dough together; let pieces fall separately.
* When all the dry flour is mixed in, press dough into a ball and flatten it.
* For best results, refrigerate dough for at least half an hour before rolling it out. If dough has been chilled for more than 1 hour let it warm up a bit before roll~ing.
* Roll out on a lightly~floured surface. Roll quickly with as few strokes as possible. If room is warm, check that dough is not sticking. Sprinkle just enough flour on top of dough to keep rolling pin from stick~ing.
* Fold crust in half, slip it gently into pie plate, and un~fold. Trim edge so that it overhangs pie plate ¼~½ inch.
* Fold edge underneath itself and flute (see page 119 for fluting illustration). If a top crust is to be added, wait to trim, fold and flute both crusts together.

Pie beans

Pie beans keep the sides of a pastry crust from slumping when the crust is pre~baked without filling.

* Line prepared crust with aluminum foil.

* Fill with 1½ c. uncooked dry beans.

* Bake as directed in specific recipe, or for 5~7 minutes in a preheated 450° oven.

* Lift beans and foil out of crust soon after removing from oven.

  * Pie beans can be reused indefinitely. Store in refrigerator or freezer.

117

Weaving a Lattice Crust

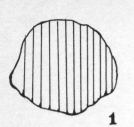

1

* Roll thoroughly chilled pie dough out on a well-floured surface.
* Cut dough into ½" wide strips (1).
* Lay six parallel strips of dough across top of filled pie. Fold every other strip back onto itself (2).
* Lay one long strip across the center of the pie, perpendicular to the others (3).
* Unfold strips back over the top of the perpendicular strip. Fold every other strip back over itself (4).
* Lay a second strip across.
* Unfold the folded strips and fold back the ones that had been lying flat.
* Continue process of laying strips across and folding and unfolding until first half of lattice is woven (5).
* Fold strips that are underneath the center cross-strip back onto themselves (6).

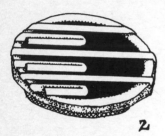

2

3

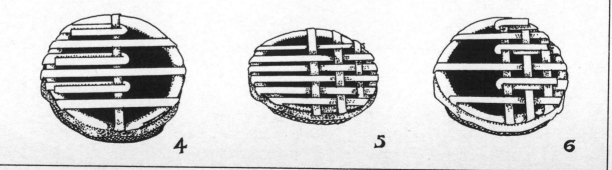

4   **5**   **6**

★Repeat same process on second side until entire lattice is woven (7).

★Using a knife or scissors, trim lattice strips and bottom crust to overhang pie plate ½".

★With lightly floured fingers, tuck edge of bottom crust up over lattice strips and pinch together (8).

★To flute edge place thumb and index finger on inside of crust with middle finger between them on the outside. Pinch inside fingers together while pressing in with middle finger (9). Keeping fingers in same formation, place index finger in hollow just formed by thumb and pinch again. Repeat process until entire edge is fluted.

★Chill pie for 10~15 minutes before brushing lattice with an egg white wash.

★Bake as directed.

7

8

9

Graham Cracker Pie Crust

1 10" pie plate
prep. 30 min.

- 2 packages (½ lb.) graham crackers
- ½ c. butter, melted
- ¼ c. honey

⭐ Finely crumb the crackers in a blender or food processor.

⭐ Mix all ingredients together and press into pie plate.

⭐ Build it up high enough around the outside to form an even edge.

Use 100% whole wheat, honey-sweetened graham crackers if available. The difference in flavor will surprise you.

Non-Dairy Graham Cracker Crumb Crust

1 9"x9" baking pan
or 1 10" springform pan
prep. 30 min.

~ Use for tofu cheesecakes.

- 1 package (¼ lb.) graham crackers
- ¼ c. oil
- 1 T. honey

⭐ Finely crumb the crackers in a blender or food processor and mix with oil and honey.

⭐ Press into the bottom of pan.

Graham Cracker Cheesecake Crust

1 10" springform pan
prep. 20 min.

- 1 package (¼ lb.) graham crackers
- ½ c. butter

⭐ Crumb graham crackers finely in a blender or food processor.

⭐ Melt butter and mix with crumbs.

⭐ Press into the bottom of pan and part way up the sides.

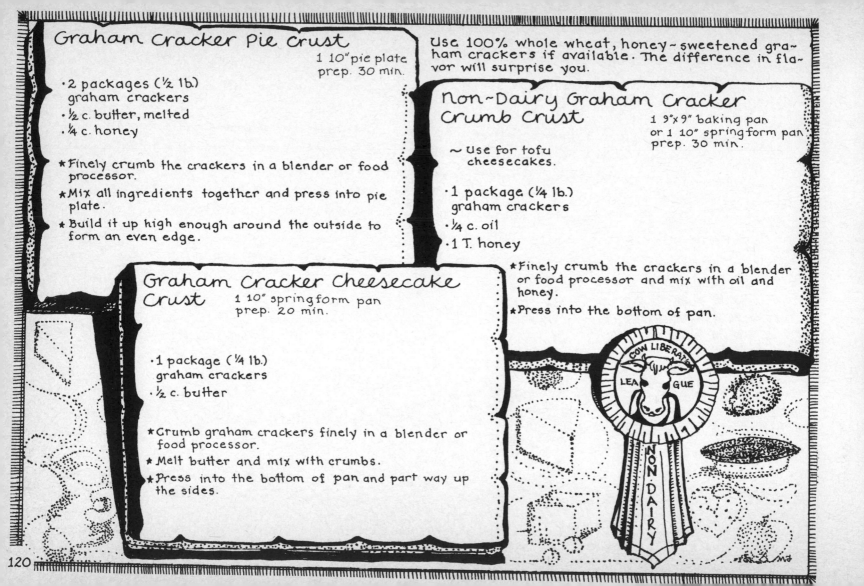

COW LIBERATION
LEAGUE
1
NON-DAIRY

Carob Crumb Crust

prep. 30 min.

A non~dairy crust suitable for Tofu Cheesecakes, page 164, and other non~dairy desserts.

For a **10"** pie plate:
- 1¼ c. whole wheat pastry flour
- ½ c. carob powder
- ¼ c. sesame seeds
- ³/₈ c. oil
- 3 T. honey

For a **9" x 9"** baking pan or **10"** round springform pan:
- ½ c. + 2 T. whole wheat pastry flour
- ¼ c. carob powder
- 2 T. sesame seeds
- 3 T. oil
- 1½ T. honey

★ Mix flour, carob powder and sesame seeds together.
★ Stir in oil and honey and blend thoroughly.
★ Press into the bottom of pan or pie plate.

Granola Crumb Crust

preheat oven to 350°
1 10" pie plate
prep. 25 min.; baking 15 min.

Use for Butterscotch Crunch Pie, page 106, or Ice Cream Pie, page 112.

- 1 package (¼ lb.) graham crackers
- 1¼ c. granola
- ³/₈ c. butter
- ⅛ c. honey

★ Finely crumb the graham crackers in a blender or food processor.
★ Pick out any large pieces of nuts or fruit from the granola, then mix it with the crumbed crackers.
★ Melt butter and mix with honey, then pour into granola~crumb mixture.
★ Press into a pie plate, building it up around the sides to make a smooth edge.
★ Bake for 15 minutes at 350° if crust is for a pie that does not require baking.

Coconut Chocolate Crust

Use for Frozen Chocolate Custard Pie, page 111, or an Ice Cream Pie, pages 112~113.

· 2 oz. unsweetened chocolate
· 1⅔ c. unsweetened shredded coconut
· 1 c. whole wheat pastry flour
· ¼ c. butter, chilled
· ⅓ c. maple syrup
· 3~4 T. cold water

★ Grate chocolate and mix with coconut and flour.

★ Grate in butter and mix it lightly.

★ Stir in maple syrup.

★ Add a bit of cold water to moisten crumbs just enough that they hold together when pressed between two fingers.

★ Press crust into pie plate.

★ Bake for 10 minutes.

preheat oven to 425°; 1 oiled 10" pie plate prep. 25 min.; baking 10 min.

Brownie Almond Crust

Recycle those old dried-out brownies you forgot to eat.

1 10" pie plate; prep 30 min.

· 4~5 large (approximately 2½" x 3½") stale chocolate brownies
· ½ c. ground toasted almonds
· ⅛ c. butter

★ Crumble brownies and mix with finely ground almonds (a blender works well for grinding).

★ Melt butter and stir into brownies.

★ Press into a pie plate.

★ Bake for 10 minutes at 350° if using a filling that does not require baking.

Cashew Oat Crust

preheat oven to 350°
1 10" pie plate
prep. 30 min.; baking 15 min.

- 1 c. rolled oats
- 1 c. cashews, finely ground, raw and unsalted if available
- 1 c. wheat germ, raw if available
- 1 t. cinnamon
- ½ c. butter (or oil)
- ⅓ c. honey

★ Mix oats, cashews, wheat germ and cinnamon together.

★ Melt butter (or heat oil) and stir in honey.

★ Combine all ingredients.

★ Press into a pie plate.

★ Bake for 15 minutes if using a filling that does not require baking.

Puddings,

Bavarian Creams,

Custards

& Crisps

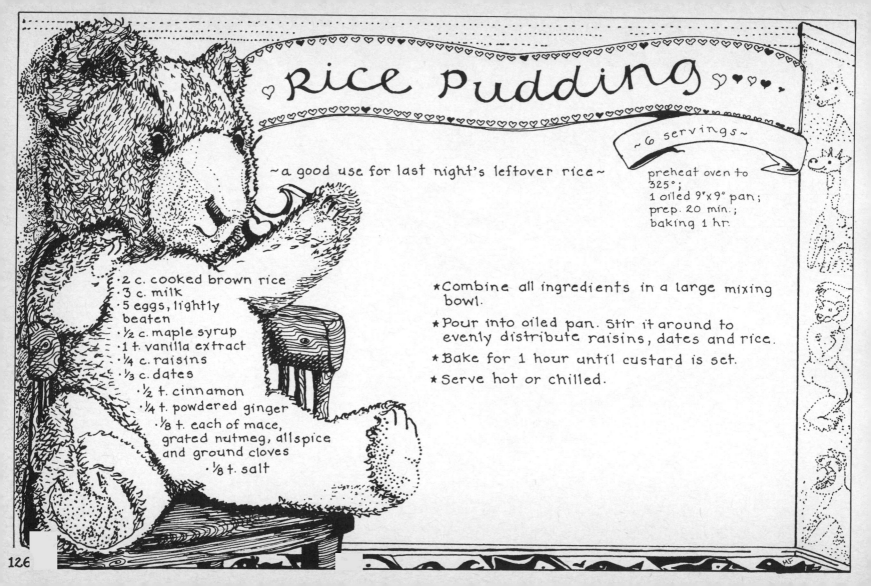

Rice Pudding

~6 servings~

~a good use for last night's leftover rice~

preheat oven to 325°;
1 oiled 9"x9" pan;
prep. 20 min.;
baking 1 hr.

- 2 c. cooked brown rice
- 3 c. milk
- 5 eggs, lightly beaten
- ½ c. maple syrup
- 1 t. vanilla extract
- ¼ c. raisins
- ⅓ c. dates
- ½ t. cinnamon
- ¼ t. powdered ginger
- ⅛ t. each of mace, grated nutmeg, allspice and ground cloves
- ⅛ t. salt

★ Combine all ingredients in a large mixing bowl.

★ Pour into oiled pan. Stir it around to evenly distribute raisins, dates and rice.

★ Bake for 1 hour until custard is set.

★ Serve hot or chilled.

Indian Spiced Rice Pudding

* Follow recipe for Rice Pudding, page 126.
* Substitute ½ c. chopped dried apples for dates.
* Add ¼ c. chopped cashews.
* Increase cinnamon to 1 t., ginger to 1½ t., allspice and cloves to ¼ t.
* Omit mace and nutmeg.
  * Add 1 t. freshly-ground cardamon.
* Bake as directed.

Apricot Orange Rice Pudding

preheat oven to 350°

* Follow recipe for Rice Pudding, page 126.
* Substitute 1½ c. orange juice for equal amount of milk.
* Reduce maple syrup to ⅓ c.
* Substitute ½ t. pure orange extract OR ½ t. ~ 1 t. grated orange rind for half the vanilla.
* Omit raisins, dates and spices.
* Add 1 c. (½ lb.) chopped dried apricots, unsulphured if available
* Add pinch ground cloves.
* Bake at 350° for 1¼ ~ 1½ hours, until custard sets.

Indian Pudding

6 servings ~ preheat oven to 350°; 1 oiled 9"x9" baking pan; prep. 20 min.; baking 1 hr.

A chance to be innovative with leftover Cornbread, page 192.

- 2½ c. cornbread, crumbled
- 6 eggs, beaten
- 3 c. milk
- ½ c. maple syrup
- ¼ c. honey
- 4 t. blackstrap molasses
- 1½ t. vanilla extract
- ¼ c. raisins
- ½ c. walnuts, chopped
- ¼ c. dates, chopped
- pinch of salt

★ Mix all ingredients together and pour into oiled pan.

★ Stir to evenly distribute the dried fruit and nuts.

★ Bake for 50 minutes to 1 hour until custard is set.

★ Serve hot or cold, plain or topped with whipped cream.

Carob Corn Pudding

prep. 20 min.; waiting 15 min.; baking 1 hr.

★ Follow Indian Pudding recipe, this page, but cut the cornbread in small cubes instead of crumbling it.

★ Add ½ c. **carob powder** to mixture.

★ Let pudding stand for 15 minutes before baking.

mf

JAMAICAN ⋆ BREAD ⋆ pudding

7 servings ~ preheat oven to 325°;
1 oiled 9"x 9" baking pan;
prep. 45 min.; baking 45~60 min.;
chilling (opt.) 1½ hr.

- 4 c. whole wheat bread, cubed (no need to remove crusts)
- 1½ c. milk
- 2 oz unsweetened chocolate
- 1 c. honey
- 1½ c. cream cheese
- 5 eggs
- 1 t. vanilla extract
- 3 T. rum
- 2 t. coffee liqueur
- ⅛ t. salt
- ½ c. currants
- ½ c. pecans, finely chopped
- 1 c. heavy whipping cream (optional)

⋆ Cut bread into small cubes and soak it in milk for 15 minutes.

⋆ Melt chocolate in a double boiler. Remove from heat and add honey to help it cool.

⋆ Beat cream cheese until smooth and fluffy.

⋆ Beat in cooled chocolate and honey, eggs, vanilla extract, rum, liqueur and salt.

⋆ Stir in soaked bread and milk.

⋆ Stir in currants and pecans.

⋆ Pour into oiled pan.

⋆ Bake for 45 minutes to 1 hour, until completely set in center of pan.

⋆ Serve hot or cold, with whipped cream.

129

Gingerbread PUDDING

7 servings ~ preheat oven to 350°;
1 oiled 9"x9" baking pan;
prep. 20 min.; baking 50 min.; chilling (opt.)
1½ hr.

- ⅓ of a 9"x13" baking pan of Walnut Gingerbread, page 79 (or any other gingerbread) to equal approximately 7 cups of gingerbread pieces. A little more or a little less won't hurt, if that's what you have.
- 6 eggs
- 3 c. milk
- ¼ c. honey
- 3 T. blackstrap molasses
- 2 T. + 1 t. ground ginger
- ¼ t. dry mustard seed, ground
- pinch salt
- ½ c. chopped walnuts or raisins or both (optional)
- 1 c. heavy cream (optional)

Freshen up that last ⅓ of a pan of gingerbread by making it into a quick bread pudding. Spicy and moist, and just asking for whipped cream, it holds the same appeal that the gingerbread started out with.

★ Break gingerbread into pieces, trying not to crumble it.
★ Beat eggs and mix with remaining ingredients, except cream.
★ Pour custard over gingerbread and stir lightly.
★ Pour into oiled pan and bake for 50 minutes.
★ Serve hot or chilled ~ topped with whipped cream.

Sweet Potato pudding

7 servings ~ preheat oven to 350°;
1 oiled 9"x 13" pan ; cooking potatoes
45 min. ; prep. 30 min. ; baking 45 min.;
chilling (opt.) 1 hr.

· 3 large sweet potatoes or yams (about
2½ lbs)
· ½ c. honey
· ½ c. maple syrup
· 1½ c. milk
· 6 eggs, separated
· 1 t. cinnamon
· 1¼ t. ground cloves
· ¼ t. grated nutmeg
· ¼ t. ground mace
· ½ c. butter, melted
· 1 t. lemon extract
· ½ c. cashews, chopped
· 1 c. heavy cream
(optional)

★Bake or boil sweet potatoes until
they are soft. Peel skins away and
then measure out 3 c. mashed potato.

★In a blender or food processor purée
measured sweet potato with honey, maple
syrup, milk, egg yolks and spices.

★Add cooled melted butter and lemon extract.

★Beat 4 egg whites to soft peaks and fold into
mixture.

★Pour into oiled pan and top with chopped
cashews.

★Bake at 350° for 45 minutes
until set.

★Serve pudding hot or cold,
topped with whipped
cream.

MF

Floating Island

5 servings ~ preheat oven to 325°;
1 oiled 9"x 9" baking pan or 5 heat-resistant custard cups ; prep. 40 min.; baking 20 min.

- 4 c. milk
- 4 eggs, separated
- ¾ c. maple syrup
- 2½ t. vanilla extract (or substitute ½ t. almond extract or brandy for 1 t. of the vanilla)
- 2 T. arrowroot mixed with 2 T. water
- ⅛ t. salt

~ A childhood favorite, this light egg custard has islands of floating meringue

★ Heat milk over medium heat until bubbles form at the edge and milk is steaming. Then remove from heat.

★ In a small bowl, lightly beat egg yolks and ½ c. of the maple syrup. Stir in a bit of the hot milk and then whisk the mixture into the rest of the milk.

★ Whisk in 2 t. of the vanilla and the arrowroot~water paste.

★ Cook over low heat for about 5 minutes, whisking constantly, until custard thickens.

★ Pour into baking pan or individual custard cups.

★ Beat 2 egg whites to soft peaks. Then beat in remaining ¼ c. of maple syrup and ½ t. of vanilla and salt.

★ Spoon egg whites onto custard and do not spread them smooth.

★ Bake for 20 minutes until meringue is golden~brown and custard is set.

★ Serve warm or chilled.

132

mm

Lemon~Lime Meringue Pudding

6 2-oz. servings ; 6 custard cups ;
prep. 1 hr. ; chilling 2 hr.

- 6 T. arrowroot
- ¼ c. water
- 1 c. maple syrup
- ⅛ t. salt
- 2 c. milk
- 4 egg yolks (save
  2 whites for meringue)
- ½ c. lemon juice

OR

- ¼ c. each lemon and lime juice
- 1 t. grated lime rind

meringue :
- 2 egg whites
- ⅓ c. maple syrup
- ⅛ t. cream of tartar

★ Mix arrowroot and water until smooth.

★ Combine with maple syrup and salt in the top of a double boiler and heat over, not in, boiling water.

★ In a second saucepan, scald milk.

★ Gradually pour milk into hot syrup, stirring vigorously with a wire whisk. Mixture should thicken immediately. Remove top of double boiler from heat and continue whisking for another minute.

★ In another bowl lightly beat egg yolks and add a bit of the hot milk. Then add yolks to milk mixture, whisking until smooth.

★ Return pudding to double boiler and cook another 5 min~ utes, whisking often.

★ Remove from heat, add lemon juice and grated lime rind, and pour into custard cups.

★ To prepare meringue, beat egg whites until they are stiff and dry. Heat syrup and cream of tartar in a small saucepan to soft ball stage, 238°~240° on a candy thermometer. Gradually pour hot syrup over egg whites, beating constant~ ly at high speed. Continue beating another minute until whites are glossy.

★ Generously spoon meringue onto pudding and place custard cups under a hot broiler for a few minutes until the me~ ringue is lightly browned.

★ Chill pudding for 2 hours before serving ; garnish with a thin slice of lemon or lime.

Dark Chocolate Pudding

- 2 c. milk
- 2 T. arrowroot
- ¼ c. unsweetened cocoa
- ½ c. honey
- ⅛ t. salt
- 1 t. vanilla extract
- 2 egg yolks
- ½ c. heavy cream (opt.)
- 2 T. walnuts (opt.)

★ Heat 1¾ c. of the milk in a double boiler.
★ Make a paste out of the remaining ¼ c. milk, arrowroot, cocoa and honey. When milk is very hot, but before it scalds, whisk in paste.
★ Then whisk in salt and vanilla.
★ Continue cooking for 10 minutes, whisking often so a skin doesn't form on the top.
★ Lightly beat egg yolks and whisk them into the custard. Cook 5 more minutes.
★ Pour into individual custard cups, garnish with chopped nuts and/or whipped cream.
★ Serve hot or chilled.

Light Chocolate pudding

★ Follow recipe for Dark Chocolate Pudding, this page.
★ Reduce **cocoa** to 2 T.
★ Reduce **honey** to ¼ c.

vanilla pudding

* Follow recipe for Dark Chocolate Pudding, page 134.
* Omit **cocoa**.
* Reduce **honey** to 3 T.
* Increase **vanilla** to 2 or 3 t.

carob pudding

* Follow recipe for Dark Chocolate Pudding, page 134.
* Substitute **4 T. carob powder** for cocoa.
* Reduce **honey** to 3 T.
  Carob pudding will not be quite as smooth as other puddings since the texture of carob powder is slightly gritty. For as smooth a pudding as possible, whip the carob paste in a blender until smooth and be sure to cook it the full 15 minutes.

Dutch Chocolate pudding

* Follow recipe for Dark Chocolate Pudding, page 134.
* Reduce **milk** to 1¾ c. and heat all of it.
* Reduce **honey** to ¼ c., **cocoa** to 3 T.
* Make paste with **¼ c. frozen orange juice concentrate**. Paste must be at room temperature to avoid curdling the milk. If pudding does curdle slightly, try whipping it in a blender or food processor and then continue cooking.
* Substitute **1 t. Grand Marnier** (an orange liqueur) for vanilla extract (optional), and whisk it into pudding after removing from heat.
* Garnish pudding with **slices of orange**.

MF

Chocolate MOUSSE

* ·4 oz unsweetened chocolate
* ·1 c. honey
* ·4 eggs, separated
* ·1 T. vanilla extract or any other sweet liqueur.
* ·3 c. heavy cream
* ·¼ t. cream of tartar
* ·grated chocolate for garnish (optional)

★Melt chocolate in a double boiler.

★Remove top pan from heat and add ¾ c. of the honey to help chocolate cool.

★In a large bowl beat egg yolks with an electric mixer for 5 minutes until light and thick.

★Beat in extract or liqueur.

★Continue beating, and add the cooled chocolate mixture a little at a time until it is all mixed together. Then beat 2 minutes more.

★Whip 1 c. cream until stiff. Add 2 T. honey and whip another minute. Then fold cream into chocolate with a rubber spatula.

★Whip egg whites until soft peaks form. Whip in cream of tartar and remaining 2 T. honey.

★Gently fold egg whites into chocolate.

★Pour into serving bowl or fill individual cups to within ½" of top. Chill in refrigerator for at least 1 hour.

★Just before serving, whip remaining 2 cups of cream until stiff and generously spoon onto chilled mousse.

Peach Melba

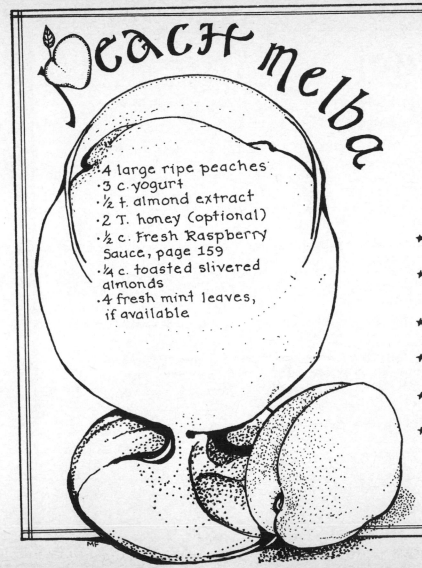

- 4 large ripe peaches
- 3 c. yogurt
- ½ t. almond extract
- 2 T. honey (optional)
- ½ c. Fresh Raspberry Sauce, page 159
- ¼ c. toasted slivered almonds
- 4 fresh mint leaves, if available

yogurt, in place of ice cream, turns this traditional dish into a light, nutritious dessert.

★ Remove skins of peaches (see process used for skinning in Peach Custard Pie, page 96)

★ Tear peaches in half, remove the pits and lay fruit, torn side up, in the bottom of four glass bowls.

★ Mix yogurt, extract and honey, and pour over fruit.

★ Prepare raspberry sauce and pour it over yogurt, swirling it in a bit with a fork.

★ Dust with slivered almonds and top with mint.

★ Refrigerate for 2~3 hours before serving to allow all the flavors to mix with each other.

MF

Mocha Bavarian Cream

10 servings ;
prep. 1½ hr. ;
chilling 4 hr.

The chilled agar-agar gel will keep for several weeks, refrigerated. Make it up ahead of time and blend with cream and egg whites as desired.

- ½ c. agar-agar flakes (see Glossary of Ingredients, page 7)
- 1½ c. strong coffee
- 1½ oz unsweetened chocolate
- 2 c. milk
- 4 eggs, separated
- ¾ ~ 1 c. maple syrup or a combination of syrup and honey
- 1 t. vanilla extract
- 1 t. coffee liqueur (optional)
- 2½ ~ 4 c. heavy cream or half and half or a combination.
- grated chocolate (optional)

* Soften agar-agar in coffee. Heat carefully and simmer for 5~10 minutes, until flakes are completely dissolved. Remove from heat, add chocolate, and whisk to blend as chocolate melts.

* In a second saucepan heat milk over medium heat until bubbles begin to appear around the edges. Lightly beat egg yolks and whisk them into hot milk. Whisk for 2~3 minutes, then remove from heat. Add sweetener, vanilla extract and liqueur.

* Combine the two mixtures in a bowl and chill for at least 4 hours until jelled.

* In small batches, whip agar-agar gel with cream in a blender or food processor until smooth, light and very thick. Use just as much cream as necessary for blending.

* Whip egg whites to soft peaks and fold them into Bavarian. Or omit egg whites for a richer, slightly heavier Bavarian.

* Pour into dessert dishes or parfait glasses. Garnish with a light sprinkling of grated chocolate and chill before serving.

MF

bavariations

Variations on Mocha Bavarian Cream. Follow recipe on the preceding page with the following substitutions:

Coffee Bavarian Cream

* Boil down **2 c. strong coffee** to equal 1½ c. stronger coffee.
* Omit chocolate.
* Garnish with **slivered almonds** or **whipped cream**.

Chocolate Bavarian Cream

* Substitute **water** for coffee.
* Increase **chocolate** to 2½ oz.
* Omit liqueur, or else substitute Amaretto or brandy.

Black Forest Bavarian Cream

* Follow Chocolate Bavarian Cream, this page. Add ¼ c. **brandy** or **Kirsch**.
* Layer Bavarian in a parfait glass with **Cherry Topping**, page 156.
* Top with **whipped cream**.

Peach Bavarian Cream

* Substitute ¾ c. **apple juice** and **1 c. puréed fresh peaches** for coffee.
* Add additional **1 c. puréed peaches** and **juice of half a lemon** to agar-agar mixture after removing it from heat.
* Omit chocolate.
* Substitute **Kirsch** for coffee liqueur.
* Decrease sweetener to ⅔ c.
* Garnish with **fresh fruit** or **slivered almonds**.

Orange Bavarian Cream

* Substitute **orange juice** for coffee. Boil 2 c. juice down to equal 1½ c., or prepare 1½ c. extra-strong from frozen concentrate.
* Omit chocolate, vanilla and coffee liqueur.
* Add **juice of 1 lemon** (about ¼ c.), **2 t. grated orange peel**, **1½ t. orange extract**, and **1 T. orange liqueur** (optional).
* Garnish with **orange slices**.

CRÈME BRÛLÉE

This elegant custard is surprisingly quick and simple to make.

6 servings ; 1 heat~resistant serving bowl or 6 heat~resistant custard cups ; prep. 35 min. ; cooling 20 min ; chilling 1~2 hr.

- 4 egg yolks (whites can be frozen. Save them for Green Mountain Frosting, page 147, a meringue, or an egg wash.)
- ⅔ c. maple syrup
- 1 pint heavy cream
- ⅓ c. maple sugar **OR** honey~sweetened apricot preserves (if available) with 1 t. apricot brandy
- 1 tray ice cubes

★ In the top of a double boiler, beat egg yolks lightly with a fork.

★ Heat (but do not boil) maple syrup and slowly whisk it into egg yolks.

★ Cook mixture over (not in) boiling water, whisking often, until thick (about 4 minutes). Cool.

★ Whip cream until stiff and fold it into cooled mixture.

★ Pour into a heat~resistant serving bowl or into indi~vidual custard cups and chill for at least 1 hour.

★ Cover chilled custard with maple sugar if available. If maple sugar candy can be found, it can be powder~ed in a blender. If maple sugar is not available, mix apricot preserves with apricot brandy and spread this on the custard.

★ Just before serving time, place baking dish or custard cups in a shallow pan and fill the pan with ice. Place pan under a hot broiler for about 30 seconds, just until the sugar carmelizes.

140

mm

Today "parfait" usually connotes ice cream in a tall glass, perhaps with a fruit or syrup swirled through it. But once, a parfait (French for "perfection") was made from frozen angelica, which is lighter and softer than ice cream.

MAPLE Parfait

Prepare this basic angelica and layer it with fresh fruit, a fruit syrup, pages 160~61, Chocolate Sauce, page 157, or a liqueur.

- 2/3 c. maple syrup
- 3 egg whites
- 1 pint heavy cream
- Candied Brandied Pecans, page 82 (optional)

* In a small saucepan boil maple syrup to thread stage, 230° on a candy thermometer.
* Beat egg whites to soft peaks. Gradually pour boiling hot syrup over whites, beating continuously. Beat several more minutes until whites are cooled.
* Whip cream until just stiff and fold into whites.
* Pour into parfait glasses or into a mold, and layer with whatever catches your fancy.
* Prepare pecans. Garnish parfaits with cooled candy and freeze.
* Remove from freezer half an hour before serving.

MF

141

Apple Crisp

12 servings~ preheat oven to 350°; 1 oiled 9"x 12" baking pan; prep. 1 hr.; baking 1~1½ hr.

Fruit:

- 12 baking apples (14 c. sliced)
- ¼ c. maple syrup
- ¼ c. honey
- 2 t. lemon juice
- 4 t. vanilla extract
- 1 T. cinnamon
- ¼ t. powdered ginger
- ⅛ t. each of grated nutmeg, ground cardamon and ground cloves
- ¼ c. butter

for Fruit

★ Peel, core and slice apples.
★ Mix with all other ingredients except butter.
★ Spread apples in oiled pan, making sure to spread them up into corners.
★ Dot apples with butter.

Topping

- 3 c. rolled oats
- 3 c. whole wheat pastry flour
- 2 t. cinnamon
- ⅛ t. each of powdered ginger, grated nutmeg, ground cardamon and ground cloves
- 1 c. butter, chilled
- ½ c. maple syrup
- 2 t. vanilla extract

for Topping

★ Prepare topping by mixing dry ingredients together. Break butter into dry mix in pea~sized pieces. Mix syrup and vanilla together and stir into dry mix.
★ Cover apples with topping.
★ Bake for 1~1½ hours, until apples are soft but not mushy and topping is lightly browned.
★ Serve hot or cold.

Strawberry Rhubarb Crisp

12 servings ~ preheat oven to 350°;
1 oiled 9"x 13" baking pan; prep. 1 hr.;
baking 50 min.

Fruit:
- 3 lbs. rhubarb (10 c. diced)
- 1 c. water
- ¾ c. honey
- 2 T. arrowroot mixed with
- 2 T. water
- 1 quart strawberries, thickly sliced

Topping:
- 3 c. rolled oats
- 3 c. whole wheat pastry flour
- 1 c. wheat germ
- 1 t. cinnamon
- pinch ground cloves
- 1 c. butter, chilled
- 1 c. honey
- 2 t. vanilla extract

★ Wash and cut rhubarb into small pieces.

★ Simmer with water in a large covered saucepan over medium heat until fruit is soft. Stir often to avoid burning.

★ Stir in honey and arrowroot and cook just a minute more.

★ Pour rhubarb into oiled pan.

★ Cover with sliced berries.

★ Mix dry topping ingredients together.

★ Cut in butter or grate it in with a large-sized grater.

★ Combine honey and vanilla and stir into topping.

★ Spread topping over fruit and bake for 50 minutes until crisp.

MF

143

Frostings, Fillings, Glazes, Toppings, Sauces & Syrups

German Coconut Frosting

6 c. frosting, enough to layer and frost 1 8" or 9" layer cake; prep. 25 min.; cooling 45 min.

- ²/₃ c. butter
- ½ c. maple syrup
- ½ c. honey
- 2 eggs
- 1⅓ c. heavy cream
- 1 t. vanilla extract
- 2²/₃ c. unsweetened shredded coconut
- 1⅓ c. walnuts, chopped

★ Combine all ingredients except coconut and walnuts in a heavy-bottomed saucepan.

★ Cook over medium heat, stirring constantly with a whisk until mixture comes to a boil and begins to thicken.

★ Remove from heat and stir in coconut and walnuts.

★ Cool to room temperature before frosting cake.

Green Mountain Frosting

6 c. frosting, enough to layer and frost 1 9" round 3-layer cake ; prep. 25 min.

A light, smooth frosting, named for the mountains of Vermont ~ great on Dark Chocolate Cake, page 38, and Dutch Chocolate Cake, page 39. Have cake cooled and ready to frost before starting to make this frosting, as it needs to be applied immediately.

- 4 egg whites
- 1 c. maple syrup
- ¼ t. cream of tartar

★ Beat egg whites until stiff.

★ Bring maple syrup and cream of tartar to a rolling boil in a small saucepan. Boil to soft ball stage, 238°~240° on a candy thermometer.

★ Begin beating egg whites again, at high speed, and slowly pour in boiling syrup. Beat continuously until all the syrup is mixed in, and then for another few minutes until egg whites have cooled down.

★ Frost cake immediately before frosting begins to harden.

mm

cream cheese frosting

3¾ c. frosting, enough to layer and frost 1 9" round layer cake; prep. 15 min.

- 1 c. unsalted butter
- 1 lb. cream cheese
- ½ c. maple syrup or honey
- 1½ vanilla extract
- ½ c. ~ 1 c. non~instant dry milk powder (optional)

★ Start with butter and cream cheese at room temperature.

★ Cream butter until completely smooth, then beat in cream cheese.

★ Beat in sweetener and vanilla extract.

★ If a stiffer frosting is needed for decorating, beat in dry milk.

★ Chill, but allow to soften slightly before frosting cake.

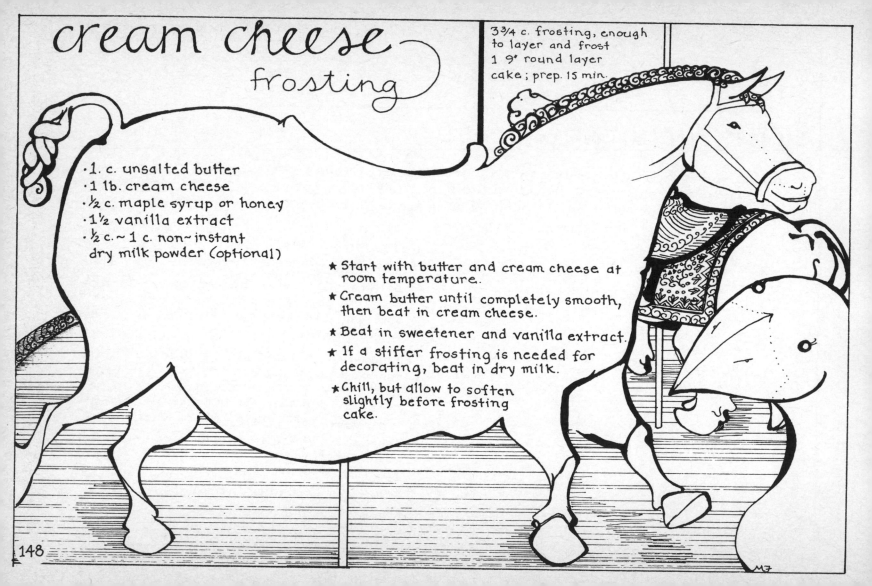

148

Chocolate Creamcheese frosting

- 3 oz. unsweetened chocolate
- ½ c. unsalted butter
- 1¾ c. cream cheese (just under 1 lb.)
- 1¼ c. maple syrup and/or honey
- 1 t. vanilla extract
- 1 T. frozen orange juice concentrate (optional)

★ Start with all ingredients at room temperature (especially the butter).

★ Melt the chocolate in a double boiler.

★ Cream butter until very soft and smooth.

★ Beat in the cream cheese until smooth.

★ Slowly beat in the sweetener, cooled chocolate, vanilla and orange juice concentrate.

★ Chill, but take out and allow to soften briefly before frosting a cake.

149

WHIPPED CREAM frosting

enough for 1 9" 3-layer cake ; prep. 5 min.

If cake is to be layered and frosted with whipped cream, use:
- 2½ c. heavy cream, chilled
- ½ t. vanilla extract
- 1 T. maple syrup

If cake is to be layered with something else, use:
- 1½ c. heavy cream, chilled
- ¼ t. vanilla extract
- 2 t. maple syrup

★ Whip cream until stiff.
★ Beat in vanilla and syrup.
★ Frost cake and refrigerate until serving time.

egg custard filling
7 c. filling; prep 30 min.; cooling 1 hr.

This custard makes a wonderful filling for both Poppy Seed Torte, page 37, and Éclairs, page 86. Use a large diameter, heavy~gauge saucepan. There's much less chance of the custard curdling if the mixture is shallow ~ only 1½~2 inches deep. It will heat more evenly and be creamier if the saucepan is heavy~gauge.

- 5 c. milk
- 2/3 c. maple syrup
- scant ½ c. honey
- 1 T. vanilla extract
- 1 c. sifted whole wheat pastry flour
- 7 eggs

* Heat milk, sweetener and vanilla on medium heat.
* Sift flour twice, sifting out and discarding the larger flecks of bran each time. Measure flour after sifting.
* Combine eggs with flour in a blender or food processor. When milk mixture begins to bubble gently, but before it scalds, whisk in eggs and flour. Continue whisking constant~ly for several minutes until custard is thick enough to coat a spoon.
* Remove from heat and cool completely before using. Bring to room temperature, stirring occasionally, before chilling, to keep a skin from forming on the top.

DATE filling
1¼ c. filling; prep. 30 min.

Use this filling for Date Bars, page 72, or Flanagan's French Toast, page 199.

- 1 c. pitted dates, pieces or chopped
- 1 c. water
- 2 t. lemon juice
- ⅛ t. each of cinnamon, powdered gin~ger and grated nutmeg
- 1 t. arrowroot mixed with 1 T. water

* Cook all ingredients except arrow~root at low heat until fairly smooth. Add extra water if necessary.
* Add arrowroot to simmering dates.
* Continue cooking until thick.

MF

marzipan filling

2¼ c. filling; prep. 30 min.;
cooling 30 min.

Use this filling to layer the Almond Torte, page 28, or Chocolate Almond Torte, page 30; in Flanagan's French Toast, pages 198~9; or in Hamentashen, page 89.

· 2¼ c. toasted almonds
· 1 c. maple syrup
· ¼ c. + 2 T. orange juice

★ Grind almonds very fine until the oil is extracted and a paste is formed. Measure out 2 c., packed, after grinding.

★ In a small saucepan bring maple syrup to a rolling boil and heat it to 235° on a candy thermometer.

★ Remove from heat and stir in almonds. Then add orange juice.

★ Cool until filling is thick and of a spreadable consistency.

Honey Almond Paste

Use this paste in recipe for Honey Almond Scones, page 188.

· ½ c. ground, toasted almonds
· 5 t. butter, melted
· 3 T. honey
· ⅛ t. almond extract (optional)

★ Grind almonds as directed for Marzipan Filling, this page.

★ Mix all ingredients together.

poppy seed filling

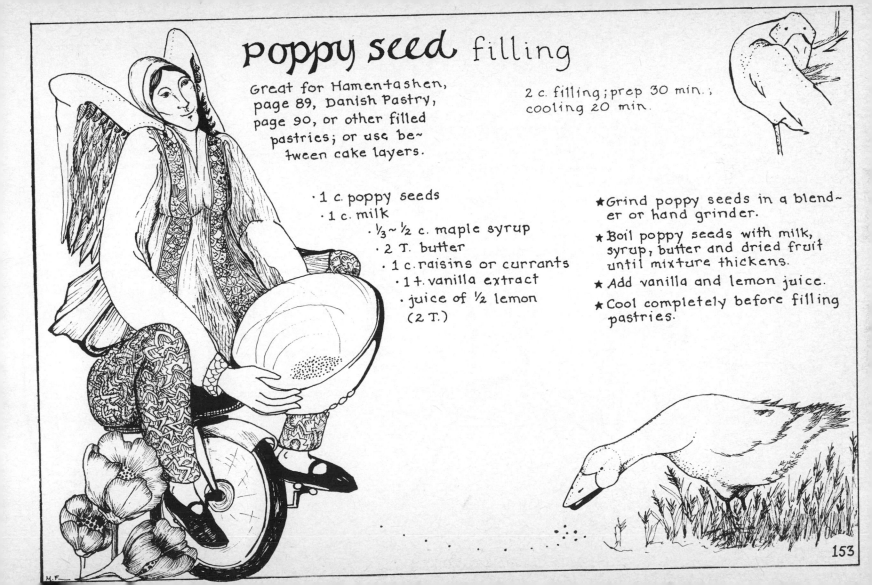

Great for Hamentashen, page 89, Danish Pastry, page 90, or other filled pastries; or use be~ tween cake layers.

2 c. filling; prep 30 min.; cooling 20 min.

- 1 c. poppy seeds
- 1 c. milk
- ⅓ ~ ½ c. maple syrup
- 2 T. butter
- 1 c. raisins or currants
- 1 t. vanilla extract
- juice of ½ lemon (2 T.)

★ Grind poppy seeds in a blend~ er or hand grinder.

★ Boil poppy seeds with milk, syrup, butter and dried fruit until mixture thickens.

★ Add vanilla and lemon juice.

★ Cool completely before filling pastries.

153

Semi-Sweet Chocolate Glaze

3/4 c. each ; prep 15 min. each

Use this glaze for Éclairs, page 86, Chocolate Strawberry Cake, page 40, Black Forest Cake, page 34, Glazed Poppy Seed Torte, page 37 or as a light coating for any fruit, cookie or pastry.

- ·2 oz. unsweetened chocolate
- ·¼ c. butter
- ·¼ c. maple syrup or honey

*Melt chocolate and butter in a double boiler.

*Add sweetener and heat for another 5 minutes.

Apple Glaze

This glaze is used for Apple Fudge Bars, page 75. It can be used to add a fruity sheen to any pastry or fruit.

- ·3/4 c. apple jelly, honey-sweetened if available
- ·¼ c. barley malt syrup (see Sweeteners, page 13)
- ·2 T. butter
- ·2 t. Kirsch (optional)

*In a saucepan bring jelly, barley malt syrup and butter to a boil.

*Boil rapidly for 4-5 minutes.

*Remove from heat and stir in liqueur if desired.

*Pour hot over pastry or fruit.

154

Honey Glaze

~ a glaze for cookies, pastries and fruit ~

1 c. each;
15 min. each

This is used as a decorative touch for a torte, page 31, and on Honey Doughnuts, page 189.

- 1 c. honey
- 1 t. lemon juice
- 2 T. butter

★ In a saucepan bring all ingredients to a rapid boil, and boil to soft ball stage, 238°~240° on a candy thermometer.

★ Remove from heat and cool a moment before pouring it onto pastry or fruit to be glazed.

★ If glazing fruit ~ make sure that fruit is very dry or else glaze will run off.

Raspberry Glaze

Use for cakes, cheesecakes, cookies and pastries.

- 10 oz raspberry preserves, honey-sweetened if available.
- 2 T. butter
- 4~6 fresh mint leaves, if available
- 1 t. any fruity liqueur or brandy (optional)

★ In a saucepan carefully bring preserves, butter and mint to a rolling boil, stirring often.

★ Boil hard for 3~4 minutes.

★ Remove from heat, stir in liqueur, and remove mint leaves.

★ Pour hot over cheesecake, cake, cookies or pastries.

155

Cherry Topping

1¾ c.; prep. 45 min.; cooling 30 min.

~ Use as toppings for tortes and cheesecakes. ~

Cherry Topping is used for Cherry Walnut Torte, page 35.

- 2 c. pitted, halved sweet cherries (a bit less than 1 lb. fresh whole cherries)
- 1 c. cherry juice and/or apple juice
- ¼ c. maple syrup
- 1 t. lemon juice
- pinch salt (optional)
- 1 T. arrowroot
- 1 T. water
- 1 T. cherry brandy or Kirsch

★ Pit, stem and halve fresh cherries if available, or use cherries frozen or canned without sugar.

★ Bring cherries and juice to a boil.

★ Add maple syrup, lemon juice and salt, and simmer gently for 4 minutes.

★ Mix arrowroot and water together and whisk into sauce. Boil for 1 more minute. Remove from heat.

★ Stir in brandy or Kirsch. Cool.

Blueberry Topping

1½ c.; prep 15 min.; cooling 30 min.

- 1 pint fresh blueberries or 10 oz frozen unsweetened blueberries
- 1 c. apple juice
- ¼ c. honey
- 1 t. lemon juice
- pinch salt
- 1 T. arrowroot mixed with 1 T. water

★ Bring blueberries, apple juice, honey, lemon juice and salt to a boil.

★ Immediately whisk in arrowroot and remove from heat.

★ Cool before using.

CHOCOLATE *sauce*

2 c.; prep 20 min.; cooling (opt.) 1 hr.

Use for Chocolate Peanut Butter Madness, page 59, or serve over ice cream.

- ·2 oz. unsweetened chocolate
- ·¾ c. water
- ·¾ ~ 1 c. honey
- ·1 T. arrowroot mixed with ¼ c. water
- ·2 T. butter
  - ·1 t. vanilla extract

*Melt chocolate in water over low heat. Stir frequently.
*Add honey and heat for a few more minutes.
*Whisk in arrowroot and whisk until chocolate thickens.
*Remove from heat and add butter and vanilla. Adjust sweetening to taste.
   *Serve hot or cold. Sauce will thicken considerably as it cools.
      *For a thicker sauce when hot, increase arrowroot by ½ t.

CAROB *orange sauce*

1 c.; prep. 15 min.; cooling (opt.) 45 min.

Try this sauce on anything you might put chocolate sauce on. It's good on ice cream or Ice Cream Pie, page 112, swirled into cheesecake or Swirled Carob Tofu Bars, page 169, or over Vanilla Pudding, page 135. Serve hot or cold.

- ·½ c. carob powder
- · 3 T. honey
- ·¼ c. frozen orange juice concentrate
- ·⅓ c. hot water
- · 1 T. butter (optional)

*Mix all ingredients in a saucepan. Adjust the sweetening to taste. Bring to a boil and whisk until smooth.

Tropical Fruit Sauce

3 c.; prep. 30 min.

~ Serve hot or cold over pancakes, waffles and ice cream.

- 20 oz. canned pineapple chunks, unsweetened
- 2 large bananas
- ½ c. orange juice
- ½ c. coconut milk

OR

- ½ c. unsweetened shredded coconut and ½ c. + 2 T. hot water *
- 2 T. rum
- ½ t. vanilla extract

★ Drain pineapple chunks, saving juice and fruit.

★ In a blender, whip bananas with pineapple juice until smooth.

★ Pour into a saucepan and add orange juice, chopped pineapple chunks and coconut milk.*

★ Simmer for 5 minutes.

★ Remove from heat and add vanilla and rum.

*If fresh coconut milk is unavailable, make a "milk" by blending shredded coconut and hot water in a blender for 4 minutes. Then squeeze "milk" out of the coconut. Discard coconut or use it in muffins, cornbread or granola.

158

Fresh Peach Sauce

~ Serve chilled with yogurt or cream, or serve hot over pancakes. Garnish with fresh mint or chopped nuts. ~

· 6 large ripe peaches
· ½ c. water
· ¼ c. honey
· ¼ t. ginger
· 2 t. Kirsch

★ Skin and pit peaches. Follow skinning process used in Peach Shortcake, page 31.

★ Purée 4 of them in a blender or food processor with the water.

  ★ Pour into a saucepan and add honey and ginger.

  ★ Bring to a boil, then remove from heat.

    ★ Stir in Kirsch.

      ★ Slice remaining peaches thinly and stir into the hot sauce.

Fresh Raspberry Sauce

~ Serve hot over ice cream, pancakes or waffles and use chilled in Peach Melba, page 137. ~

· 1 c. fresh or (frozen unsweetened) raspberries
· 1 c. orange juice
· 2 T. maple syrup
· ½ t. brandy (optional)
· 2 t. arrowroot
· 1 T. water

★ Whip raspberries and orange juice in a blender or food processor until smooth.

  ★ Pour into saucepan and add maple syrup and brandy.

  ★ Cook over medium heat until fruit begins to boil.

  ★ Mix arrowroot and water and whisk into hot sauce.

  ★ Whisk until smooth, then remove from heat.

  ★ Serve hot or cold.

  ★ For a smoother, clearer sauce pour blended fruit through a piece of cheesecloth to separate out the raspberry seeds.

Cherry Syrup

- 3 c. whole cherries, or 1 16-oz. can of pitted cherries packed in water
- ½ c. fruit juice (or water from canned cherries)
- ½ c. maple syrup
- 1 t. arrowroot
- 1 T. water
- 2 t. cherry brandy or liqueur

★ Pit cherries and sieve them through a food mill to separate out skins.

★ In a saucepan bring puréed cherries, juice and maple syrup to a rolling boil.

★ Mix arrowroot and water and whisk into boiling fruit mixture.

★ Boil for 5 minutes total; then remove from heat and whisk in cherry brandy.

★ Use fruit syrups hot or chilled.

★ Pour syrups over ice cream, pancakes or waffles, swirl them into custards and parfaits, or use them in recipes calling for maple syrup for a surprisingly fruity flavor.

★ For a refreshing summer drink, mix chilled syrups with sparkling mineral water.

syrups

Strawberry

1½ c.; prep. 20 min.

- 1 pint fresh or frozen unsweetened straw~berries
- ½ c. water
- ½ c. maple syrup

★ Purée fruit with water in a blender. Add syrup.

★ Bring to a rolling boil and boil hard for 5 minutes.

★ Remove from heat.

Blueberry

1½ c.; prep. 30 min.

- 2 c. fresh or frozen unsweetened blue~berries
- 1 c. water
- ½ c. maple syrup
- ½ t. lemon juice
- 1 t. arrowroot mixed with 1 T. water (optional)

★ Bring blueberries and water to a boil; then remove from heat.

★ Sieve through a food mill to remove skins. Then return fruit to saucepan.

★ Add maple syrup and lemon juice and boil hard for 5 minutes.

★ For a thicker syrup, whisk in arrowroot at last minute.

MF

CHOCOLATE TOFU
cheesecake

10~12 servings ~ preheat oven to 350°;
1 10" springform pan ; prep. 30 min.;
baking 45 min.

Bound to seduce chocolate lovers ~ even those most skeptical of non~dairy desserts.

- 1 Non~Dairy Graham Cracker Crust, page 120
- 18 oz. firm tofu, if available
- ⅓ c. unsweetened cocoa
- 3 medium~sized bananas
- 1 c. maple syrup
- ½ c. water
- 4 t. lemon juice
- 1 T. vanilla extract
- pinch salt
- ½ c. tahini

★ Prepare crust and press it into the bottom of a 10" springform pan or a 10" pie plate.

★ Whip all ingredients except tahini in a blender or food processor until smooth and light. Blend in several small batches.

★ Stir tahini in by hand, as it tends to gum up the blender.

★ Pour filling over crust slowly so as not to stir up crumbs.

★ Bake at 350° for 45 minutes until firm.

Banana Orange Tofu Cheesecake

★ Follow recipe for Chocolate Tofu Cheesecake, this page.
★ Omit **cocoa**.
★ Reduce **maple syrup** and **water** to ⅜ c. each.
★ Add ⅜ c. **frozen orange juice concentrate**.
★ Add a pinch of freshly-grated **nutmeg**.
★ Serve plain or top with fresh fruit or a fruit topping.

orange tofu

Bavarian Cream

* Simmer agar~agar and water over medium heat, whisking constantly until agar~agar is completely dissolved and liquid is reduced to ⅓ cup.

* Whisk in maple syrup.

* Remove from heat and whisk in orange juice.

* Whip mixture in a blender or food processor.

* Add crumbled tofu, oil, lemon extract and orange peel; continue blending 3~5 minutes until complete~ly smooth.

* Pour into parfait glasses and garnish with a slice of orange.

* Chill two hours before serving.

- 2 T. agar~agar flakes (see Glossary of Ingredients, page 7
- 1 c. water
- ¾ maple syrup
- 1½ c. orange juice
- 8 oz tofu, firm if available
- ¼ c. oil
- ¼ t. pure lemon extract
- ½ t. ground orange peel

165

Tahini Sandwich Cookies

COOKIE:

- ¾ c. tahini
- ⅔ c. honey
- ⅓ c. barley malt syrup (see Sweeteners, page 13)
- ½ t. salt
- 3 c. rolled oats
- 1 c. sunflower seeds, unsalted and raw

★ Mix tahini and sweet~ eners together. If barley malt syrup is unavailable, substitute honey, though it will change the texture of the cookie. ★ Stir in salt. ★ Combine oats and sunflower seeds and stir in wet in~ gredients. ★ Chill dough for at least 30 min~ utes to make it more manageable (as it will be very sticky). ★ Drop teaspoons of cookie dough onto an oiled cookie sheet and flatten with the palm of your hand. ★ Bake for about 10 minutes until edges are golden. Remove from oven. ★ Cool for 1~2 minutes, then move cookies to a cooling rack so they don't harden onto cookie sheet. ★ Spread cooled cookies with a thick layer of filling and top with a second cookie.

FILLING:

- ½ c. carob powder
- ⅓ c. honey
- ½ c. peanut butter
- 1 c. tahini

★ Mix filling ingredients together and stir until smooth.

~This cookie can make a whole meal in itself. It is high in protein and very filling.

Sesame Seed chews

1½ ~ 2 lbs. candy ~ preheat oven to 300°; 1 oiled 9"x 9" baking pan; prep. 35 min.; cooling 45 min.

~ a nutritious, chewy candy ~

- ¾ c. unsweetened, shredded coconut
- 1½ c. sesame seeds
- ¼ c. wheat germ
- ½ c. tahini
- ¼ c. peanut butter
- 1 c. barley malt syrup (see Sweeteners, page 13)

* Toast coconut, sesame seeds and wheat germ in oven until lightly browned. Stir occasionally.
* Blend tahini and peanut butter to~ gether.
* Bring barley malt syrup to a rolling boil at high heat. Lower heat but con~ tinue to boil rapidly for 2~3 minutes.
* Remove from heat and stir in tahini and peanut butter mixture.
* Stir in toasted ingredients.
* Spread into oiled pan. Smooth the edges with a rubber spatula.
* Cool. Cut into triangles or bars before candy is completely hardened.

167

Carob sesame COOKIES

40 cookies ~ preheat oven to 350°; 1 oiled cookie sheet; prep. 45 min.; baking 30 min.

- 2 c. sesame seeds
- 1 c. carob powder
- 2 t. baking powder
- ½ t. salt
- 1 c. whole wheat pastry flour

- 1 c. barley malt syrup
  (see Sweeteners, page 13)

- 1 c. oil

★ Mix dry ingredients together.

★ Heat barley malt (but don't boil it), and mix in oil.

★ Mix wet and dry ingredients together and stir well. Batter will be quite stiff.

★ Drop by level tablespoons onto an oiled cookie sheet and flatten them with the palm of your hand.

★ Bake at 350° for 8~10 minutes.

★ Remove cookies from cookie sheet before they cool or they may harden permanently on the sheets. Cool them on another flat surface.

These cookies have loving~ly been called "asphalt cookies" by friends, and they do indeed have a look about them of a freshly tarred road surface, but it has nothing to do with the taste. These cookies are delightfully crunchy and not overly~sweet. Add ⅓ c. honey if you want them sweeter.

168

Swirled Carob Tofu bars

12 2"x 3" bars ~ preheat oven to 350°; 1 oiled 9"x 9" baking pan; prep. 30 min.; baking 35 min.

- 1 Non~Dairy Crumb Crust, page 120 or page 121.
- 12 oz tofu, firm if available
- ¼ c. maple syrup
- 2 average~sized bananas
- juice of ½ lemon
- 1½ T. vanilla extract
- ¼ c. frozen orange juice concentrate
- ¼ c. water
- ⅜ c. tahini
- pinch salt
- ½ recipe of Carob Orange Sauce, page 157; reduce water in sauce to 1 T. and omit butter

* Prepare crumb crust and press it into the bottom of an oiled 9"x9" baking pan.

* Blend all ingredients in a blender or food processor until light and smooth.

* Pour onto unbaked crust.

* Prepare carob sauce and swirl it into the filling.

* Bake at 350° for 25~35 minutes until set.

fruity CHEWS

- 1 c. dried apples
- 1 c. raisins
- ¼ c. boiling water
- ¾ c. walnuts
- ¾ c. sunflower seeds, unsalted and raw if possible
- 1 c. pitted dates
- 3 T. lemon juice
- ⅔ c. unsweetened shredded coconut

★ Soak apples and raisins in boiling water for 15 minutes until soft.

★ Grind walnuts and seeds finely.

★ Purée the soaked fruit. Add just enough of the soaking water as needed to mash fruit without watering it down. Fruit should make a very thick paste.

★ Chop dates finely, or purée with other fruit.

★ Mix together all ingredients except coconut. Roll mixture into small (¾" ~ 1") balls, using the palms of your hands.

★ Whip coconut in a blender until it is partially powdered.

★ Roll balls in coconut and they're ready to eat!

This recipe requires a food processor, juicer or grinder for puréeing dried fruit. A blender doesn't work because too much water has to be added to facilitate blending.

These chewy balls are naturally sweetened by fruit, and contain no added sweetener.

Cracker Jills

~ a quick sweet treat and a favorite party snack for children ~

1 lb. candy ~ preheat oven to 350°; prep. 45 min.

- 1 c. peanuts or filberts
- ½ c. popcorn (unpopped)
- 2 T. oil
- ¼ c. peanut butter
- 1 T. blackstrap molasses
- ½ c. maple syrup
- ½ c. honey

★ Toast nuts in a 350° oven for 25~30 minutes.

★ Pop popcorn in oil.

★ Mix popcorn and nuts together in a large mixing bowl.

★ Mix together peanut butter and molasses and set aside.

★ Bring maple syrup and honey to a rolling boil in a small saucepan. Cook on high heat to 250° on a candy thermometer.

★ Remove from heat, quickly blend in peanut butter and molasses, and pour hot glaze over popcorn and nuts.

★ Stir until nuts and corn are well-coated.

★ Continue stirring as candy cools to keep it from all sticking together.

★ Store in an airtight container in the refrigerator.

171

Banana Walnut muffins

This muffin is light and moist and is also suitable for those on special diets. It contains no dairy products or eggs and can also be made without any wheat flour.

1 doz. large muffins ~ preheat oven to 400°; prep. 35 min.; baking 35 min.

- 1 c. rolled oats
- 1¼ c. apple cider or juice
- 6 oz. tofu, firm if available
- ¼ c. oil
- ¼ c. honey
- 1 c. chopped banana (1½~2 large bananas)
- ¾ c. walnuts, chopped
- 1 c. sifted **whole wheat flour** and 1 c. **rice flour OR** 2 c. sifted **whole wheat pastry flour OR** 1 c. **buckwheat flour** and 1 c. **rice flour**
- 4 t. baking powder
- ⅛ t. salt

★ Mix oats and juice together.

★ Crumble tofu into a blender or food processor, and whip with oil and honey until light and creamy. Add to oats and juice.

★ Add bananas and walnuts to mixture.

★ In a separate bowl mix flour(s), baking powder and salt.

★ Combine dry and wet ingredients, stirring briefly. Spoon into oiled muffin tin.

★ Bake at 400° for 10 minutes, then reduce heat to 350° and bake for 20~30 minutes more. Muffins are done when no indentation is left when centers are pressed.

172

fruit parfait

6 servings ~ prep. 1 hr.;
chilling 1~2 hr.

An elegant, refreshing fresh fruit dessert for a hot summer day. Develop your own favorite combinations of fruit.

- 4 T. agar~agar flakes (see
  Glossary of Ingredients, page 7)
- 2 c. apple juice
- 1 c. orange juice or other
  sweet fruit juice
- 4 large peaches or 2½ c.
  purée of other fresh fruit
- juice of 1 lemon (¼ c.)
- 1~2 t. fruity liqueur
  (optional)
- ½ recipe Fresh Raspberry
  Sauce, page 159, or any
  other fresh fruit sauce
  with a contrasting color
  to the whipped fruit
- mint leaves, if available

* Boil agar~agar in apple juice, whisking often,
  until agar~agar is completely dissolved and
  liquid is reduced to 1½ c.
* Whisk occasionally as it begins to cool and gel.
  Do not let the gel become solid before complet-
  ing the next step. This may only take 8~10 minutes.
* Whip orange juice, peaches, lemon juice and
  liqueur in a blender until smooth, then add
  mixture to agar~agar.
* Whip it in blender or food processor in small
  batches until light and smooth.
  Fill 6 oz. parfait glasses half full.
* Spoon on 2~3 T. cooled raspberry sauce,
  then fill glasses to the top.
* Garnish with fresh mint leaves and berries.
* Chill at least one hour before serving.

Banana buckwheat muffins

~ see page 20 ~

1 doz. large muffins ~ preheat oven to 400°; prep. 40 min.; setting 2 hr. or overnight; baking 25 min.

Soak oats in wet ingredients overnight for a moist, light muffin.

· 3 eggs
· ¼ c. apple cider or juice
· ½ c. yogurt
· ⅓ c. peanut oil or melted butter
· ¼ c. honey
· 3 bananas
· 1 c. rolled oats

· 1 c. buckwheat flour
· 1 c. whole wheat pastry flour
· 4 t. baking powder

★ Beat eggs.
★ Beat in cider, yogurt, oil and honey.
★ Chop bananas and add to mixture.
★ Stir in rolled oats.
★ Set overnight, or at least a few hours.
★ Then preheat oven to 400°.
★ Mix dry ingredients together, then combine with wet. Stir briefly.
★ Spoon batter into oiled muffin tin, filling cups to the brim.
★ Bake at 400° for 10 minutes, then reduce temperature to 350° and bake an additional 15 minutes, until centers of muffins are firm.

176

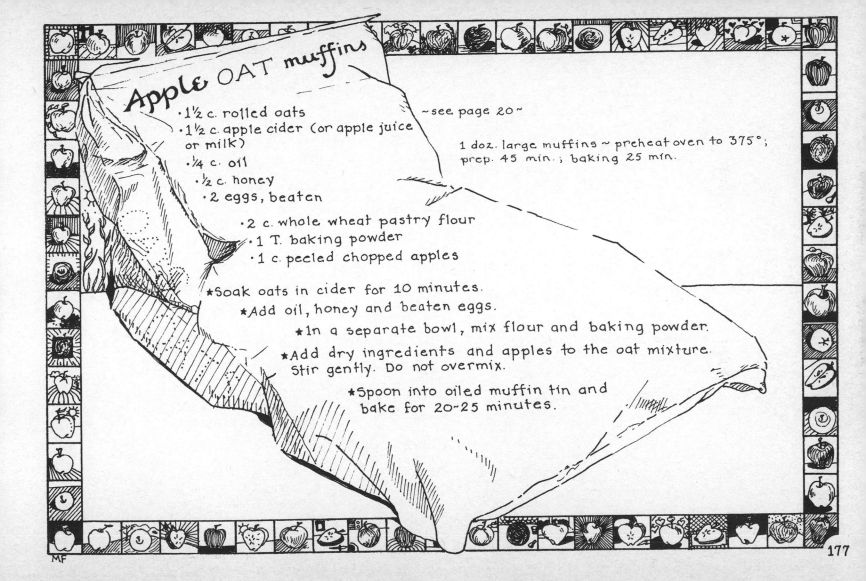

Apple OAT muffins

- 1½ c. rolled oats
- 1½ c. apple cider (or apple juice or milk)
- ¼ c. oil
- ½ c. honey
- 2 eggs, beaten

~ see page 20 ~

1 doz. large muffins ~ preheat oven to 375°; prep. 45 min.; baking 25 min.

- 2 c. whole wheat pastry flour
- 1 T. baking powder
- 1 c. peeled chopped apples

★Soak oats in cider for 10 minutes.

★Add oil, honey and beaten eggs.

★In a separate bowl, mix flour and baking powder.

★Add dry ingredients and apples to the oat mixture. Stir gently. Do not overmix.

★Spoon into oiled muffin tin and bake for 20~25 minutes.

MF

Bran Date muffins

~see page 20~

~see page 20~

1 doz. large muffins ~ preheat oven to 350°; prep. 30 min. ; baking 30 min.

· 1½ c. bran
· 1½ c. apple cider or juice
· ½ c. blackstrap molasses
· 2 eggs, beaten
· ¼ c. oil

· 2 c. whole wheat pastry flour
· 1 T. baking powder
· ½ t. salt
· 1 c. chopped dates

★ Soak bran in juice for 10 minutes.

★ Add molasses, beaten eggs and oil, mixing thoroughly.

★ In a separate bowl mix 1¾ c. of the flour, baking powder and salt.

★ Dredge date pieces in the remain~ ing ¼ c. flour. This helps keep dates from sinking to the bottom of muffins.

★ Combine all ingredients together ~ just until moist. Don't overmix!

★ Spoon into well ~ oiled muffin tin, filling cups to top.

★ Bake 25 ~ 30 minutes.

MOLASSE

178

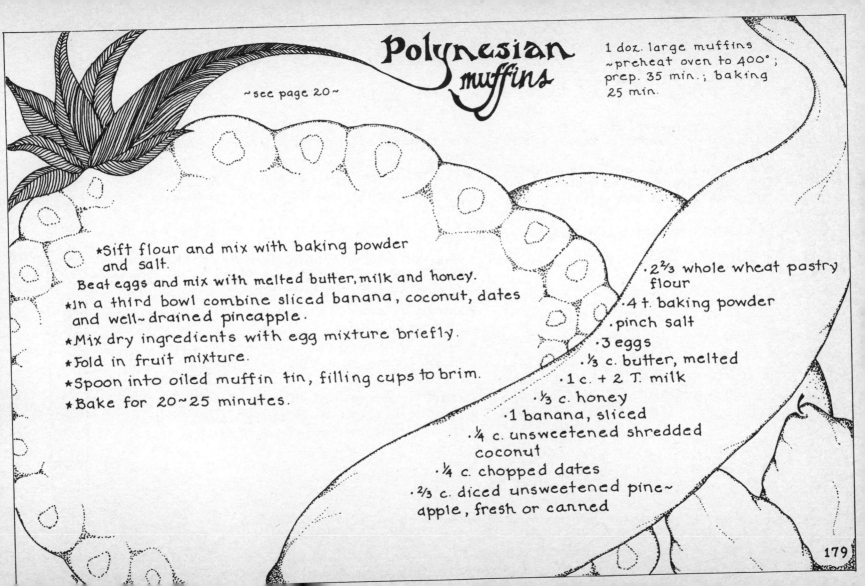

Polynesian muffins

~see page 20~

1 doz. large muffins
~preheat oven to 400°;
prep. 35 min.; baking
25 min.

*Sift flour and mix with baking powder and salt.

Beat eggs and mix with melted butter, milk and honey.

*In a third bowl combine sliced banana, coconut, dates and well~drained pineapple.

*Mix dry ingredients with egg mixture briefly.

*Fold in fruit mixture.

*Spoon into oiled muffin tin, filling cups to brim.

*Bake for 20~25 minutes.

· 2⅔ whole wheat pastry flour
· 4 t. baking powder
· pinch salt
· 3 eggs
· ⅓ c. butter, melted
· 1 c. + 2 T. milk
· ⅓ c. honey
· 1 banana, sliced
· ¼ c. unsweetened shredded coconut
· ¼ c. chopped dates
· ⅔ c. diced unsweetened pine~apple, fresh or canned

179

Any muffins

~see page 20~

1 doz. large muffins ~
preheat oven to 400°;
prep. 30 min.; baking 25 min.

This never~fail muffin recipe serves as the base for many excit~ ing variations. Make them plain or try the suggestions that follow. Then have fun creating your own; the possibilities are infinite.

· 2¾ c. whole wheat pastry flour
· 4 t baking powder
· pinch salt

· 3 eggs
· ⅓ c. butter
· 1 c. milk
· ¼ c. honey } or 1¼ c. fruit juice
· ¾ c. fresh or dried fruit, nuts, or a combination*

*If adding fruit that is very juicy, like strawberries or peaches, re~ duce the amount of milk or fruit juice by ¼ c.

★ Sift together the flour, baking powder and salt.

★ In a separate bowl, beat the eggs.

★ Melt the butter and let it cool; then add it to the eggs.

★ Add milk and sweetener or fruit juice to the eggs.

★ Mix wet and dry ingredients together brief~ ly. The secret to light muffins is to stir the batter as little as possible.

★ Gently fold in ¾ c. of fruit, nuts or anything else you choose.

★ Spoon into an oiled muffin tin, filling cups to the brim, and bake at 400° for 20~25 minutes.

★ Muffins are done when center peaks are firm to the touch. If muffins don't peak, either the oven temperature is too low or the batter is too runny.

ricotta raspberry
muffins
~see page 20~

* Follow recipe for Any Muffins, page 180.
* Add **1 t. almond extract** to wet ingredients.
* Swirl **½ c. raspberry jam** (honey-sweetened if available) into mixed batter.
* Fill muffin tins half full. Spoon in ½ t. **each of ricotta cheese and raspberry jam**. Fill muffin tins with remaining batter.
* Bake at 400° for 10 minutes. Reduce oven temperature to 350° and bake 10 more minutes.

peanut butter and jelly
muffins
~see page 20~

* Follow recipe for Any Muffins, page 180.
* Reduce **milk** to ¾ c.
* Reduce **butter** to 3 T.
* Add **¾ c. peanut butter** to melting butter and blend together.
* Add **¾ c. jelly or jam** (honey-sweetened if available) to the wet ingredients, breaking jelly into small specks.
* Bake at 375° for 25 minutes.

~see page 20~

~see page 20~

Spicy Apple Carrot muffins

* Follow recipe for Any Muffins, page 180.
* Add ⅛ t. allspice, ¼ t. nutmeg and ½ t. cinnamon to dry ingredients.
* Grate 1 apple to make ½ c. grated apple; drain well.
* Grate 1 large carrot to make ¾ c. grated carrot.
* Combine apple and carrot with batter just before spooning into muffin tin.

Corn Date muffins

* Follow recipe for Any Muffins, page 180.
* Reduce flour to 1 c.
* Add 2 c. unrefined cornmeal to dry ingredients.
* Increase baking powder to 5 t.
* Mix ¾ c. chopped dates into dry ingredients just before combining with wet ingredients.

Almond Bran
Apple Cheddar
muffins

★ Follow Any Muffins recipe, page 180.

★ Reduce **flour** to **2 c.**

★ Add ¾ c. **bran** and 1½ c. **ground toasted almonds** to dry ingredients.

★ Add ¾ t. **almond extract** to wet ingred~ients.

~see page 20~

★ Follow recipe for Any Muffins, page 180.

★ Add ¾ c. **grated sharp cheddar cheese** and ¾ c. **peeled grated apples** (or chop-ped dried apples) to batter just before spooning into muffin tin.

★ Bake at 400° for 10 minutes, then re~duce oven temperature to 350° and bake 10~15 minutes more.

~ see page 20 ~

Lemon BLUEBERRY
muffins

~see page 20~

1 doz. large muffins ~ preheat oven to 400°; prep. 25 min.; baking 20 min.

- 2¼ c. whole wheat pastry flour
- ¾ c. unrefined cornmeal
- 5 t. baking powder
- ½ t. salt

- 3 eggs, lightly beaten
- 6 T. butter, melted
- 1 c. orange juice
- ¼ c. maple syrup
- 1 T. pure lemon extract
- ½ lb. blueberries, fresh or unsweetened frozen, drained

★ Mix dry ingredients together.

★ Mix wet ingredients together.

★ Dredge blueberries in 1 T. of the dry mix.

★ Combine all ingredients, stirring very briefly.

★ Fill muffin tins to full.

★ Bake at 400° for 20 minutes until tops are firm.

MF

~ Record your own muffin innovations here.

honey almond scones

- 1 c. rolled oats
- ½ c. yogurt
- 1 T. honey
- 1 T. butter, melted
- 3 T. water
- 1 egg, lightly beaten

- 1½ c. whole wheat pastry flour
- ½ c. rye flour
- 2 t. baking powder
- ¾ t. baking soda
- ⅛ t. salt
- Honey Almond Paste, page 152

★ Whip ½ c. of the rolled oats in a blender or food processor until mostly powdered, and mix with yogurt, honey, melted butter, water, and lightly beaten egg.

★ Mix ½ c. of the pastry flour with all the rye flour, baking powder, baking soda and salt.

★ Stir the wet ingredients into the dry ingredients. Add enough pastry flour so that the dough can be kneaded for a couple of minutes.

★ Flatten and shape into a disc measuring about 7 inches in diameter and about 1½ inches thick. Use extra oats to keep dough from sticking.

★ Coat loaf with more rolled oats and place on a baking pan that is lined with oats.

★ Cut ½ inch deep slashes so that loaf is marked in quarters.

★ Bake at 400° for 10 minutes; then reduce oven temperature to 350° and bake an additional 10~15 minutes.

★ While scone is baking, prepare the almond paste. Spread paste on hot scone and cut into 8 pieces.

Honey Doughnuts

- 1½ t. baking yeast
- ½ c. warm water
- ½ c. milk
- ¼ c. oil
- 1 T. molasses + honey to equal ½ c.

- 4½ c. sifted whole wheat pastry flour
- ¼ t. salt
- 2 t. cinnamon
- 2 t. powdered ginger
- ½ t. ground cloves
- 6~8 c. oil for frying
- Honey Glaze, page 155 (optional)
- ⅓ c. walnuts, chopped (optional)

~flavorful and fun~

* Dissolve yeast in water. Set in a warm place until yeast begins to bubble (5~10 minutes).
* In a second bowl combine milk, 2 T. of the oil, molasses and honey.
* In a third bowl combine dry ingredients. Save out ¼ c. flour for rolling.
* Stir liquids into dissolved yeast. Then stir in dried ingredients. Dough should be just dry enough to form into a ball. It will still be sticky. Flouring hands will facilitate handling.
* Set ball of dough in an oiled bowl. Cover dough with more oil and set in a warm place to rise for 50 minutes.
* Punch dough down, hitting it with fist 15~20 times.
* Re~form into a ball, cover with oil again and set it to rise for 30 more minutes.
* Roll dough out on a heavily floured surface to ½" thick. Cut with a doughnut cutter or 2 different~sized round cookie cutters.
* Let rounds rise on the floured surface for 30 minutes. Meanwhile, heat oil in a saucepan to 375°.
* Transfer dough to hot oil on a metal spatula. Fry for 1 minute, then turn and cook second side for 1~1½ minutes. Cook two or three doughnuts at a time and adjust heat to keep oil temperature constant.
* Drain fried doughnuts on absorbent paper.
* Prepare honey glaze as directed. Using tongs, dip doughnuts into hot glaze. Set glazed dough~ nuts on waxed paper until glaze cools. Sprinkle with chopped nuts, if desired, while glaze is still soft.

Banana walnut bread

10 slices ~ preheat oven to 350°;
1 oiled 9"x 5" loaf pan; prep. 40 min.;
baking 1 hr.

The natural fruity sweetness of the bananas shines through in this bread. For best re~ sults use overripe bananas. If they are not available you may want to add 1-2 T. more honey. This banana bread is good for breakfast or at any other time of the day!

- ¼ c. butter
- 3 eggs
- 1 t. vanilla extract
- 1 ⅓ mashed bananas (3 large bananas)
- ⅓ c. honey

- 2 c. whole wheat pastry flour
- 1 t. baking soda
- 2 t. baking powder
- ¼ t. grated nutmeg
- ½ c. walnuts, coarsely chopped

★ Start with all ingredients at room temper- ature.

★ Cream the butter until smooth, then beat in eggs and vanilla.

★ Purée mashed bananas with honey in a blend~ er or food processor, then beat into butter.

★ Mix flour with baking powder and soda and nutmeg.

★ Combine dry and wet ingredients; then stir in walnut pieces and pour into oiled pan.

★ Bake for 45 minutes to 1 hour.

★ Cool slightly before slicing.

peach walnut bread

It's a wonderful surprise to find the del- icate flavor of peaches in this bread.

★ Follow recipe for Banana Bread, this page.
★ Substitute 1 ⅓ c. puréed (3 large) peaches for bananas. Peeling peaches is unneces- sary. Increase **honey** by **1 T.** unless peaches are very sweet.

DATE nut bread

10~12 slices ~ preheat oven to 350°;
prep 50 min.; baking 1 hr.

- 2 c. + 1 T. whole wheat pastry flour
- ¼ c. wheat germ
- 1½ t. baking powder
- ½ t. baking soda
- pinch salt
- ¼ c. butter
- ½ c. honey
- 2 T. blackstrap molasses
- ¾ c. milk
- ¼ c. half and half or heavy cream
- 1 c. dates
- ½ c. pecans
- ½ c. cashews } or a combination of other nuts and seeds

* Start with ingredients at room temperature.

* Sift 2 c. of the flour and mix it with other dry ingredients.

* Cream butter, honey and molasses.

* Slowly beat in milk and cream.

* Chop dates. Dredge them in 1 T. of flour.

* Chop nuts finely.

* Add flour mix to wet ingredients. Beat until smooth.

* Stir in dates and nuts.

* Pour into oiled loaf pan and bake 50 minutes to 1 hour.

* Cool 10 minutes before slicing.

MF

191

cornbread

- 2½ c. unrefined yellow cornmeal
- 2⅓ c. whole wheat pastry flour
- 1 T. baking powder
- ⅔ t. salt
- 2½ c. milk
- 4 eggs
- ⅔ c. oil
- ⅓ c. honey

★ Mix dry ingredients together in a large mixing bowl.

★ Mix wet ingredients in a second bowl, then pour wet mix into dry ingredients.

★ Stir briefly, but do not beat out all the lumps.

★ Bake in a preheated oven for 30~35 minutes until golden brown and firm to the touch.

Yogurt Coffee Cake

8 servings ~ preheat oven to 350°;
1 oiled 9"x 5"x 2½" loaf pan or 1 2~qt. bundt
pan; prep. 30 min.; baking 1 hr.

- ½ c. butter
- ¾ c. honey
- 2 eggs
- 1 t. vanilla extract
- 2 t. almond extract
- 2 c. whole wheat pastry flour, sifted
- 2 t. baking powder
- 1 c. plain yogurt
- ½ c. chopped walnuts or almonds (optional)
- ⅓ c. maple syrup or maple sugar
- 1 t. cinnamon

★ Start with all ingredients at room temperature.

★ Cream butter, then beat in honey.

★ Beat in eggs and extracts.

★ Mix flour and baking powder, then stir into butter alternately with yogurt.

★ Add nuts.

★ Pour half the batter into an oiled pan.

★ Mix maple syrup or sugar with cinnamon and dribble ½ of this mixture into the pan.

★ Add the remaining batter and top with remaining cinnamon mixture.

★ Bake at 350° for 1 hour.

MF

Cinnamon~Raisin ENGLISH MUFFINS

1½ doz. large muffins; prep. 1 hr.;
rising 3¼ hr.; grilling 25~35 min.

~ Rich with the nutty flavor of whole wheat. ~

- 1 T. baking yeast
- ½ c. honey
- ¼ c. blackstrap molasses
- 1½ c. hot water
- 1½ c. warm milk
- 6½ c. whole wheat bread flour
- 1½ t. cinnamon
- 1 t. salt
- ½ c. butter, melted
- 1 c. raisins
- 1½ c. whole wheat bread flour for kneading
- 2 T. oil for bowl and dough
- 1 c. unrefined cornmeal for grilling

* In a large bowl, dissolve yeast, honey and molasses in water and milk. Let mixture stand for 5~10 minutes until the yeast bubbles up to the top.

* Add 4 cups of flour and stir with a wooden spoon (100~200 strokes) to incorporate air into the dough.

* Let dough rise in a warm place for 45 minutes to 1 hour, until doubled in size.

* Stir in cinnamon, salt, butter and raisins.

* Stir in 2½ cups more flour until dough comes away from sides of bowl.

Continued on next page.

* Knead for 10 minutes, adding more flour to board as needed. Dough should be very soft and moist and a bit sticky. Too much flour will make dough dry and stiff.
* Put kneaded dough in an oiled bowl. Cover dough with more oil and let it rise for 50 minutes to 1 hour until doubled in size.
* Punch dough down and let it rise again for 40 minutes.
* Roll out dough on a floured board to ¾" thick and cut into 4" rounds.
* Let rounds rise for 30 more minutes.
* Set a grill on low to moderate heat, or use a heavy frying pan on a low flame.
* Sprinkle cooking surface with cornmeal and place muffins on it.
* Turn often, until lightly browned and cooked through, about 25~35 minutes.
* Cool muffins on a rack.
* Break muffins open with the prongs of a fork just before using.
* Freeze whatever will not be eaten in 1 or 2 days.

For a non~dairy muffin, substitute water for milk and oil for butter.

COMMON GROUND
Granola

~wonderfully crunchy and not overly sweet~

- .12 c. rolled oats
- .⅔ c. sunflower seeds (raw and unsalted)
- .1 c. almonds
- .1 c. cashews
- .1 c. unsweetened shred-ded coconut
- .½ c. sesame seeds

- .1 c. oil
- .⅜ c. honey
- .⅜ c. maple syrup
- .¼ t. vanilla extract
- .1 c. raisins

★ ★ ★ ★

*Mix dry ingredients together in a large bowl.

*In a small saucepan combine oil, honey, maple and van~illa. Heat over low heat until mixture is warm enough to blend together.

*Pour wet mix into dry ingredients and mix thoroughly. The secret to a crunchy granola is to make sure that every particle is completely coated with liquid.

*Spread mixture into 2 or 3 large baking pans and toast in low oven for 1 hour and 10 min~utes. Stir every 10 or 15 minutes. Granola is done when golden brown. Remove from oven and stir in raisins.

*Cool completely in pans, then store in an airtight container and refrigerate.

Apple-Spice Granola

★ Follow recipe for Common Ground Granola, page 196.

★ Add ½ T. cinnamon, ⅛ t. ginger, ⅛ t. allspice and a pinch of cloves to liquid mixture.

★ Substitute ⅛ t. lemon extract for vanilla extract.

★ Substitute 1 c. chopped dried apples for raisins.

Date-Nut Granola

★ Follow recipe for Common Ground Granola, page 196.

★ Add ⅔ c. chopped walnuts to dry ingredients.

★ Substitute almond extract for vanilla extract.

★ Substitute 1 c. chopped dates for raisins.

Three-Grain Granola

★ Follow recipe for Common Ground Granola, page 196.

★ Use 6 c. rolled oats.

★ Add 3 c. wheat flakes and 3 c. rye flakes to dry mixture.

MF

FLANAGAN'S
french toast

A cream cheese ~ French toast sandwich.
The cream cheese moistens the bread on the in~
side while the egg batter crisps it on the outside.

- 8 slices whole wheat bread
- ½ lb. cream cheese
- 3 eggs
- ½ c. milk
- ¼ t. cinnamon
- pinch grated nutmeg

* Make four cream cheese sandwiches.

* Beat eggs, then beat in milk and spices.

* Dip sandwiches into egg batter. Fry them, in butter or oil, on a griddle or in a heavy skillet. Use moderate heat to cook toast slowly so the cream cheese has time to warm~ about 5 minutes per side. When first side is golden brown, flip and fry the second side.

* Serve with maple syrup or a hot fruit syrup, pages 160~61.

* Try the filling suggestions on the next page.

mm

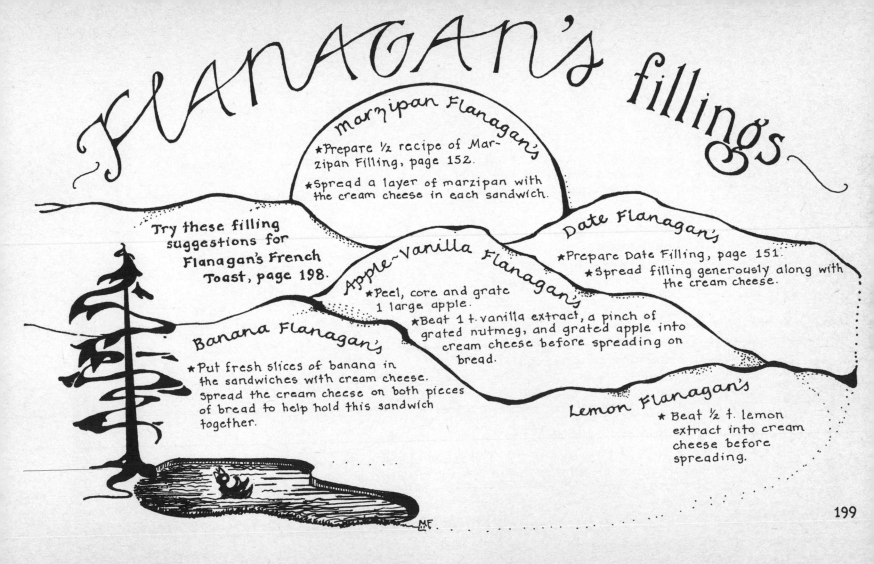

FLANAGAN's fillings

Marzipan Flanagan's
★ Prepare ½ recipe of Marzipan Filling, page 152.
★ Spread a layer of marzipan with the cream cheese in each sandwich.

Try these filling suggestions for Flanagan's French Toast, page 198.

Date Flanagan's
★ Prepare Date Filling, page 151.
★ Spread filling generously along with the cream cheese.

Apple~Vanilla Flanagan's
★ Peel, core and grate 1 large apple.
★ Beat 1 t. vanilla extract, a pinch of grated nutmeg, and grated apple into cream cheese before spreading on bread.

Banana Flanagan's
★ Put fresh slices of banana in the sandwiches with cream cheese. Spread the cream cheese on both pieces of bread to help hold this sandwich together.

Lemon Flanagan's
★ Beat ½ t. lemon extract into cream cheese before spreading.

199

Hot Cocoa

- 6 c. milk
- 1 c. water
- ⅓ unsweetened cocoa
- ½ c. maple syrup
- ½ t. cinnamon
- 1 t. vanilla extract
- ½ c. heavy cream (optional)
- ⅛ t. grated nutmeg

★ Scald milk.

★ In a double boiler heat water, cocoa, maple and cinnamon. Whisk until cocoa dissolves.

★ Whisk in scalded milk and continue cooking for 10 minutes.

★ Remove from heat and stir in vanilla.

★ Serve topped with whipped cream and a dash of nutmeg.

Hot Carob

- 1 c. water
- ⅜ c. maple syrup
- ½ c. carob powder
- ½ t. cinnamon
- ¼ t. ground cardamon
- 6 c. milk
- 1 t. vanilla extract

★ Bring water, maple syrup, carob powder and spices to a simmer over medium heat.

★ Add milk and heat slowly until very hot, but not boiling.

★ Remove from heat and stir in vanilla.

★ Serve steaming hot.

Carob is naturally sweet, and requires less added sweetening than cocoa. carob powder does not dissolve as completely as cocoa, however, and tends to settle at the bottom of cup. Serve with a spoon and stir while drinking.

Spiced Breakfast
TEA

6 c. of tea;
prep. 30 min.

- 6 c. water
- 20 pods of cardamon
- 30 whole cloves
- 2 4" sticks of cinnamon
- 20 black peppercorns
- ½" x 3" piece of fresh ginger root
- 2½ T. black tea leaves
- ¼ c. honey, or more to taste
- 1 c. milk (optional)

★ Bring water to a boil.
★ Add cardamon seeds, cloves, cinnamon sticks, peppercorns, and chopped ginger root, and simmer gently for 15 minutes, covered.
★ Remove from heat, add tea leaves, and steep for 5 minutes, covered.
★ Strain tea leaves and spices out of tea.
★ Add honey to taste.
★ Heat milk in a second saucepan until it is steaming, and add to tea.
★ Drink tea while it is steaming hot.

Index

*Bold numbers
indicate main recipes.*

R